SOARING
A STORY OF COURAGE

Written by **SUNEEL RAM**

Art, Ink, Colors and Lettering by
FANTOONS ANIMATION STUDIOS

Zuiker Press

Los Angeles

SOARING: A STORY OF COURAGE

Author photographs © 2022 Suneel Ram

Written by Anthony E. Zuiker
Art, Ink, Colors and Lettering by Fantoons Animation Studios
Designed by Roberta Melzl
Edited by Jeremy Townsend

Founders: Michelle & Anthony E. Zuiker
Publisher: David Wilk

Published by Zuiker Press
16255 Ventura Blvd.
Suite·#900
Encino, CA 91436
United States of America

Visit us online at www.zuikerpress.com

ISBN 978-1-947378-34-6 (paperback)
ISBN 978-1-947378-33-9 (hardcover)
ISBN 978-1-947378-35-3 (eBook)

PRINTED IN CANADA
February 2023

DEDICATED TO ... every young person who needs to be reminded they are not alone.

HOPE lies within these pages.

ZUIKER
PRESS

... is a husband and wife publishing company that champions the voices of young authors. We are an **ISSUE-BASED** literary house. All of our authors have elected to tell their personal stories and be ambassadors of their cause. Their goal, as is ours, is that young people will learn from their pain and heroics and find **HOPE**, **CHANGE**, and **HAPPINESS** in their own lives.

TEACHER'S CORNER

SHANNON LIVELY

is a National Board Certified educator with a bachelor's degree in elementary education from the University of Nevada, Las Vegas, a master's degree from Southern Utah University, as well as advanced degrees in differentiated instruction and technology. In 2013, she was awarded the Barrick Gold One Classroom at a Time grant, and then chosen as Teacher of the Year. She is currently teaching fifth grade at John C. Vanderburg Elementary School in Henderson, Nevada.

WHY WE HONOR TEACHERS

We understand the amount of hard work, time and preparation it takes to be a teacher! At Zuiker Press, we have done the preparation for you. With each book we publish, we have created printable resources for you and your students. Our differentiated reading guides, vocabulary activities, writing prompts, extension activities, assessments, and answer keys are all available in one convenient location. Visit Zuikerpress.com, click on the For Educators tab, and access the **DOWNLOADABLE GUIDES** for teachers. These PDFs include everything you need to print and go! Each lesson is designed to cover Common Core standards for many subjects across the curriculum. We hope these resources help teachers utilize each story to the fullest extent!

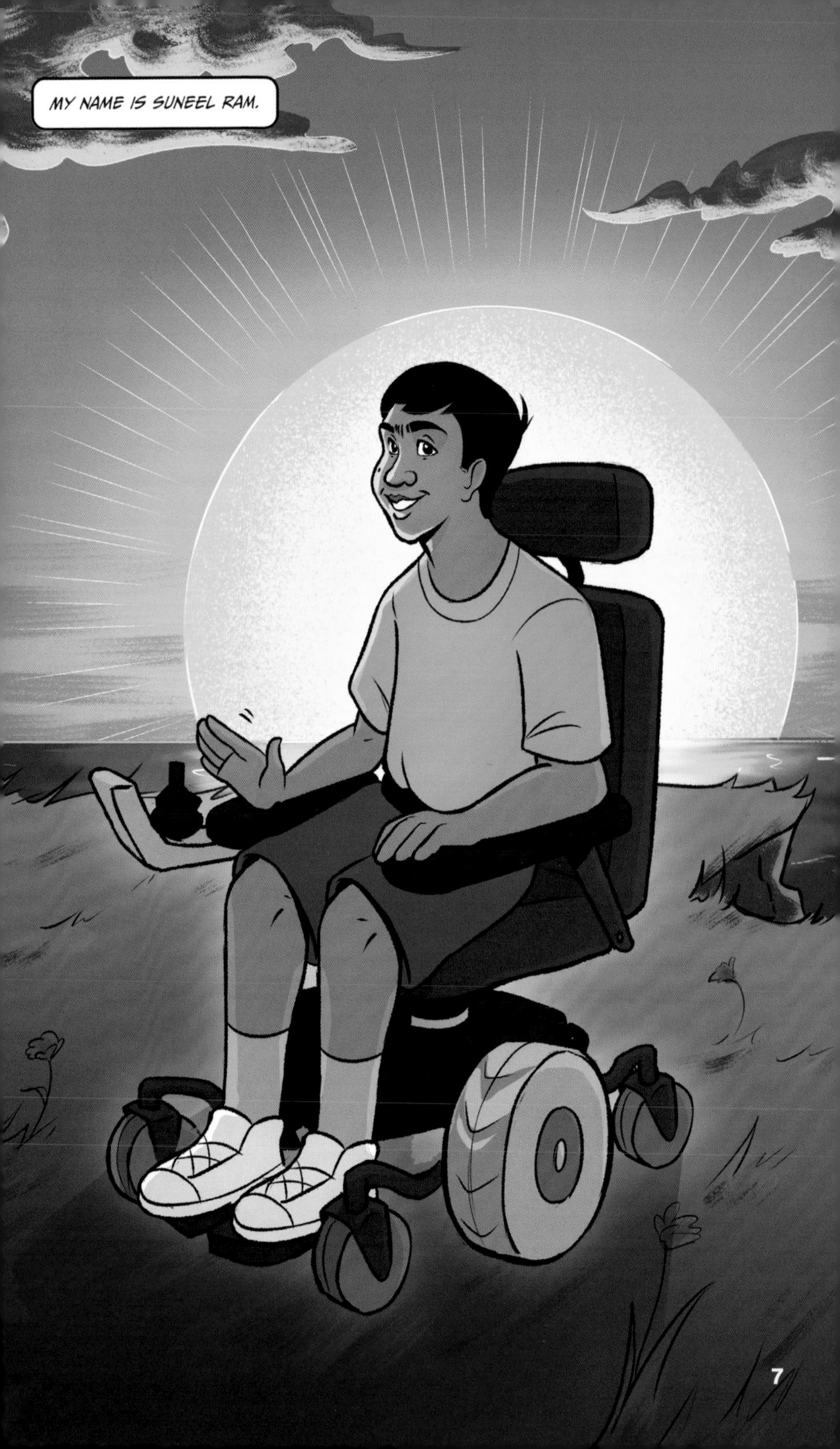
MY NAME IS SUNEEL RAM.

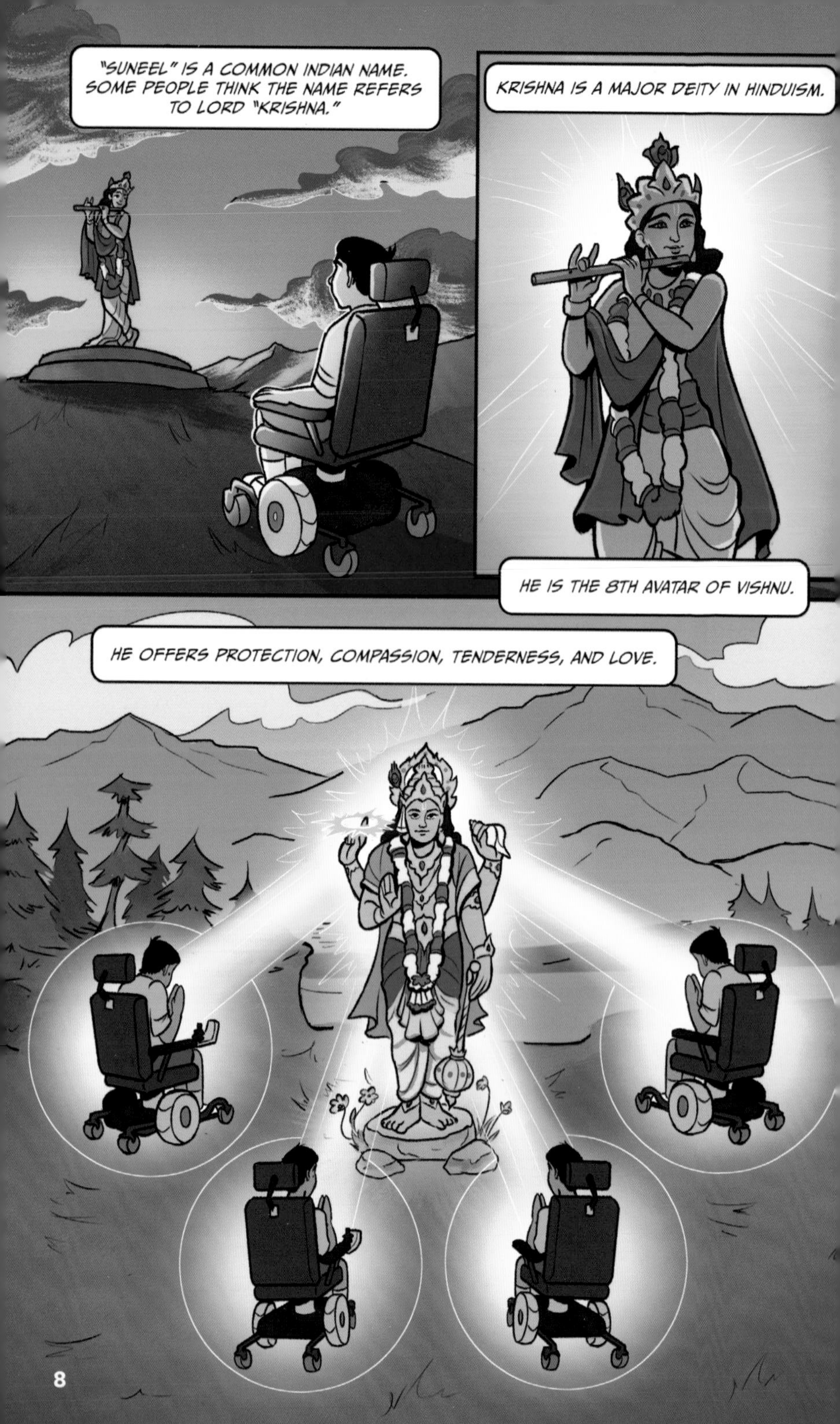
"SUNEEL" IS A COMMON INDIAN NAME. SOME PEOPLE THINK THE NAME REFERS TO LORD "KRISHNA."
KRISHNA IS A MAJOR DEITY IN HINDUISM.
HE IS THE 8TH AVATAR OF VISHNU.
HE OFFERS PROTECTION, COMPASSION, TENDERNESS, AND LOVE.

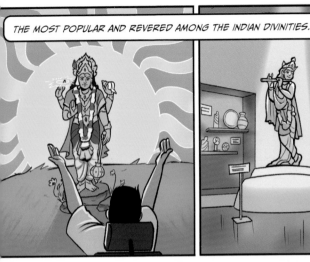

THE MOST POPULAR AND REVERED AMONG THE INDIAN DIVINITIES.

SO I GUESS THE QUESTION IS...

HOW DOES A NAME LIKE "SUNEEL", WHICH STANDS FOR SUCH GREATNESS, HAVE TO ENDURE SOME OF LIFE'S MOST DIFFICULT CHALLENGES?

IT'S A QUESTION I OFTEN ASK MYSELF IN THE STILLNESS OF MY OWN SILENCE...

9

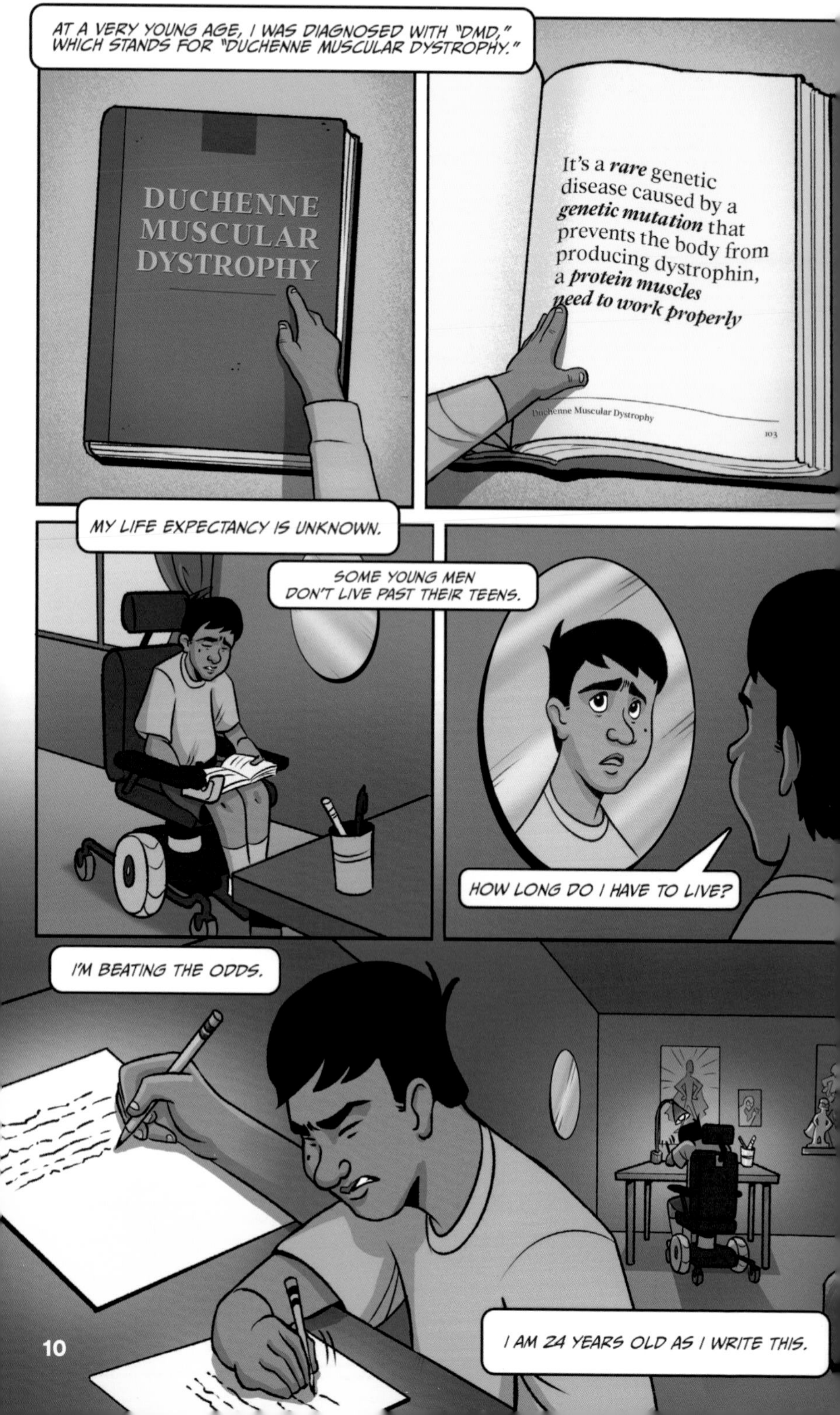
AT A VERY YOUNG AGE, I WAS DIAGNOSED WITH "DMD," WHICH STANDS FOR "DUCHENNE MUSCULAR DYSTROPHY."
DUCHENNE MUSCULAR DYSTROPHY
It's a rare genetic disease caused by a genetic mutation that prevents the body from producing dystrophin, a protein muscles need to work properly
Duchenne Muscular Dystrophy
103
MY LIFE EXPECTANCY IS UNKNOWN.
SOME YOUNG MEN DON'T LIVE PAST THEIR TEENS.
HOW LONG DO I HAVE TO LIVE?
I'M BEATING THE ODDS.
I AM 24 YEARS OLD AS I WRITE THIS.

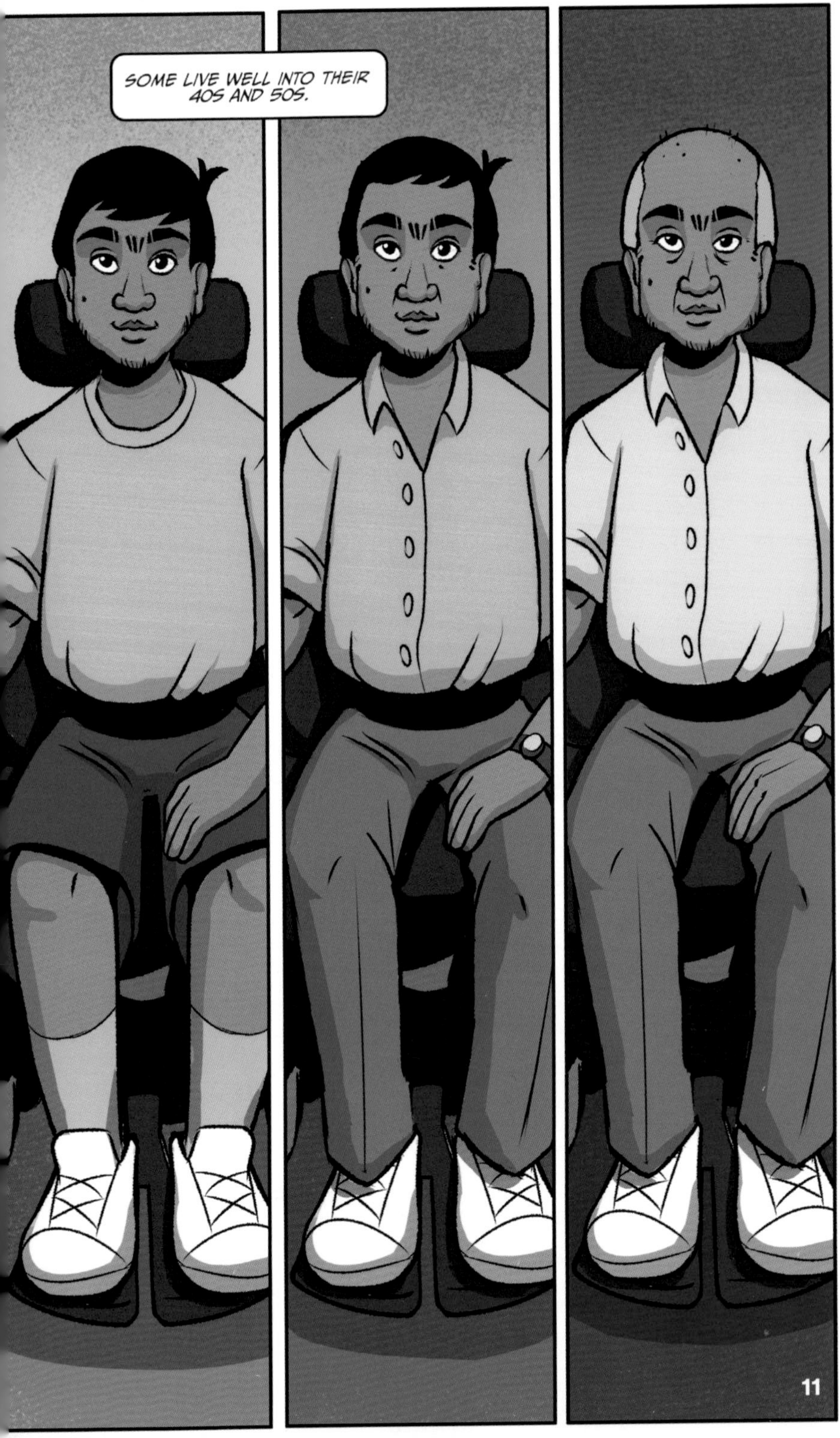
SOME LIVE WELL INTO THEIR 40S AND 50S.

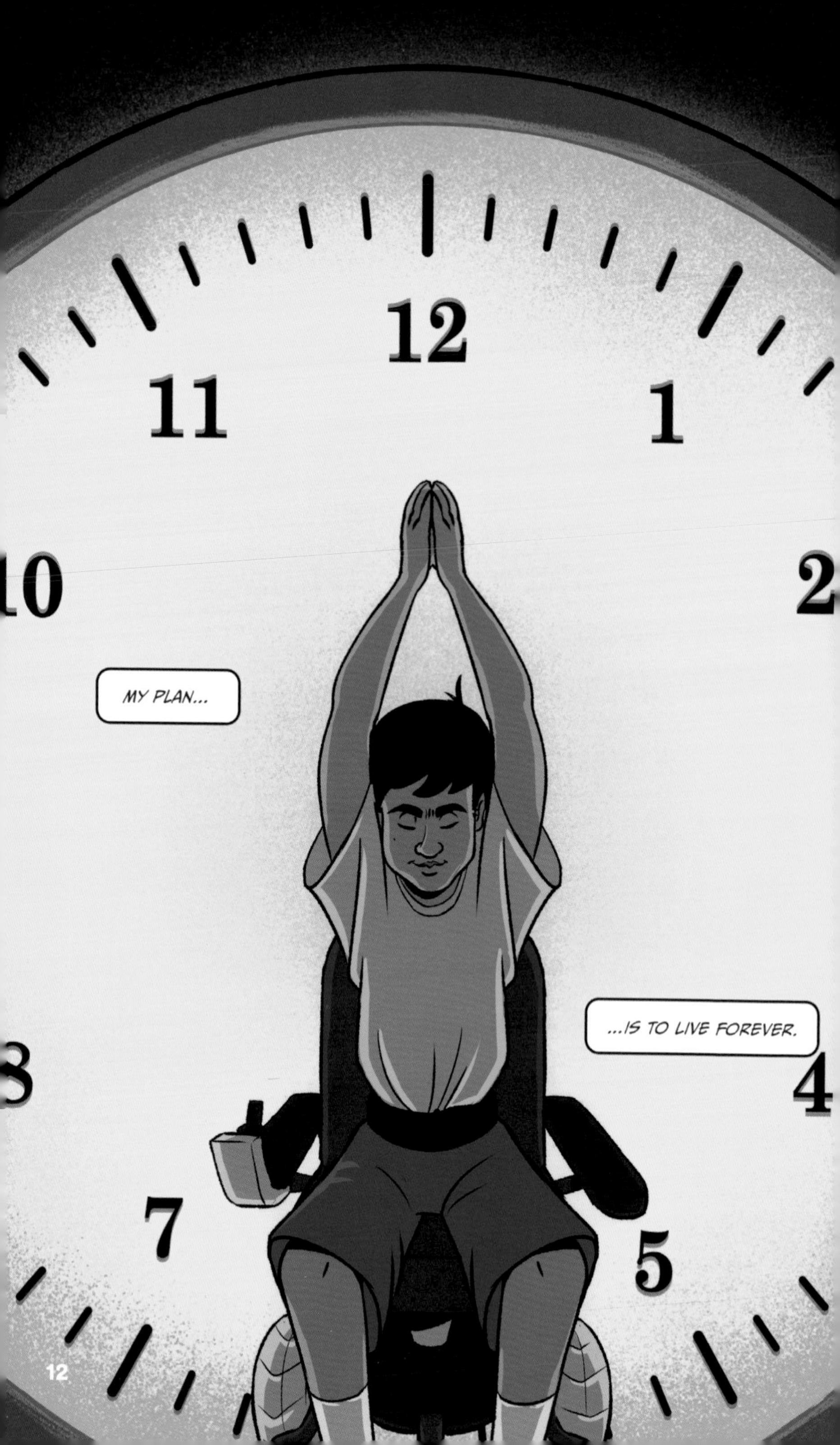
MY PLAN...
...IS TO LIVE FOREVER.

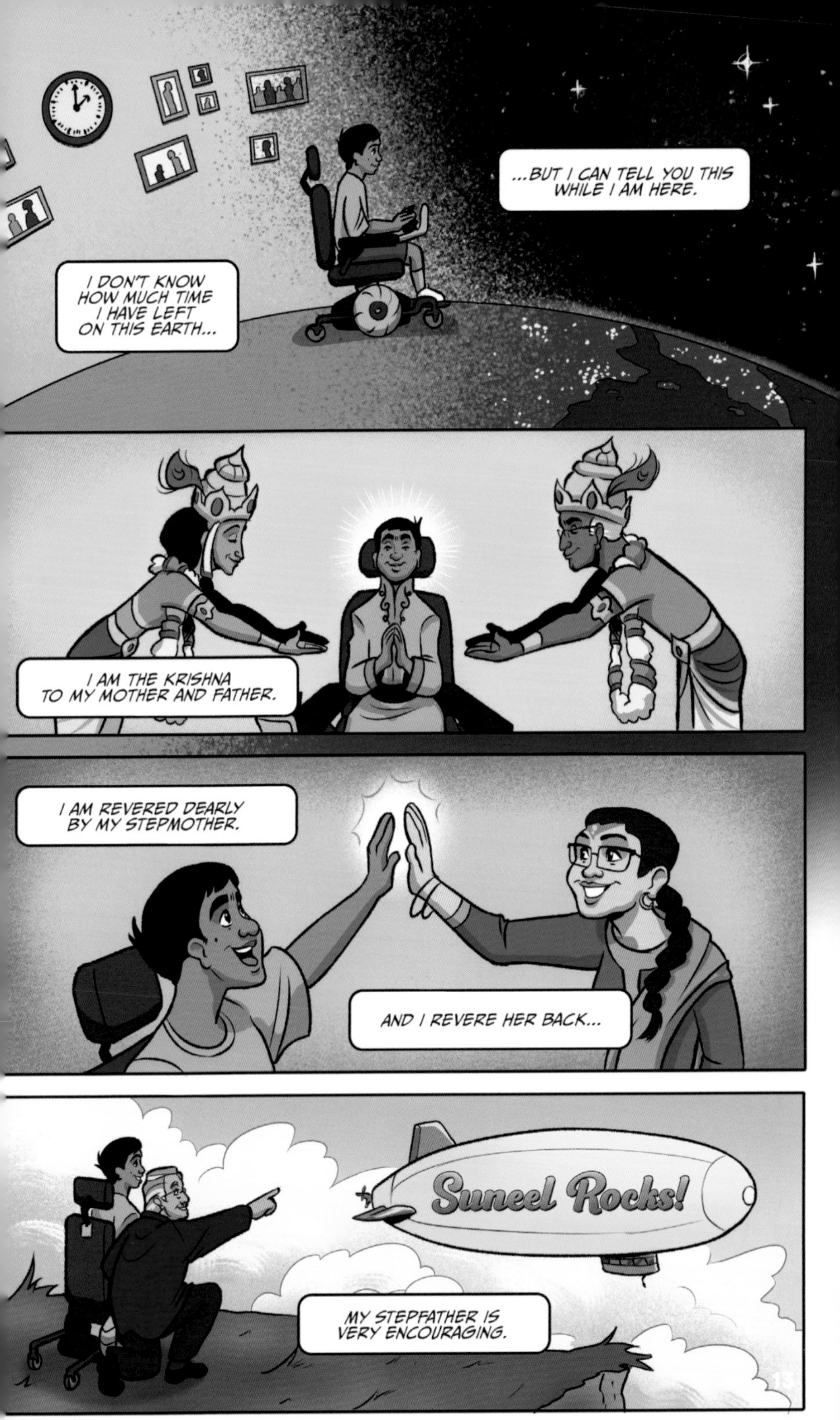
I DON'T KNOW HOW MUCH TIME I HAVE LEFT ON THIS EARTH...
...BUT I CAN TELL YOU THIS WHILE I AM HERE.
I AM THE KRISHNA TO MY MOTHER AND FATHER.
I AM REVERED DEARLY BY MY STEPMOTHER.
AND I REVERE HER BACK...
Suneel Rocks!
MY STEPFATHER IS VERY ENCOURAGING.

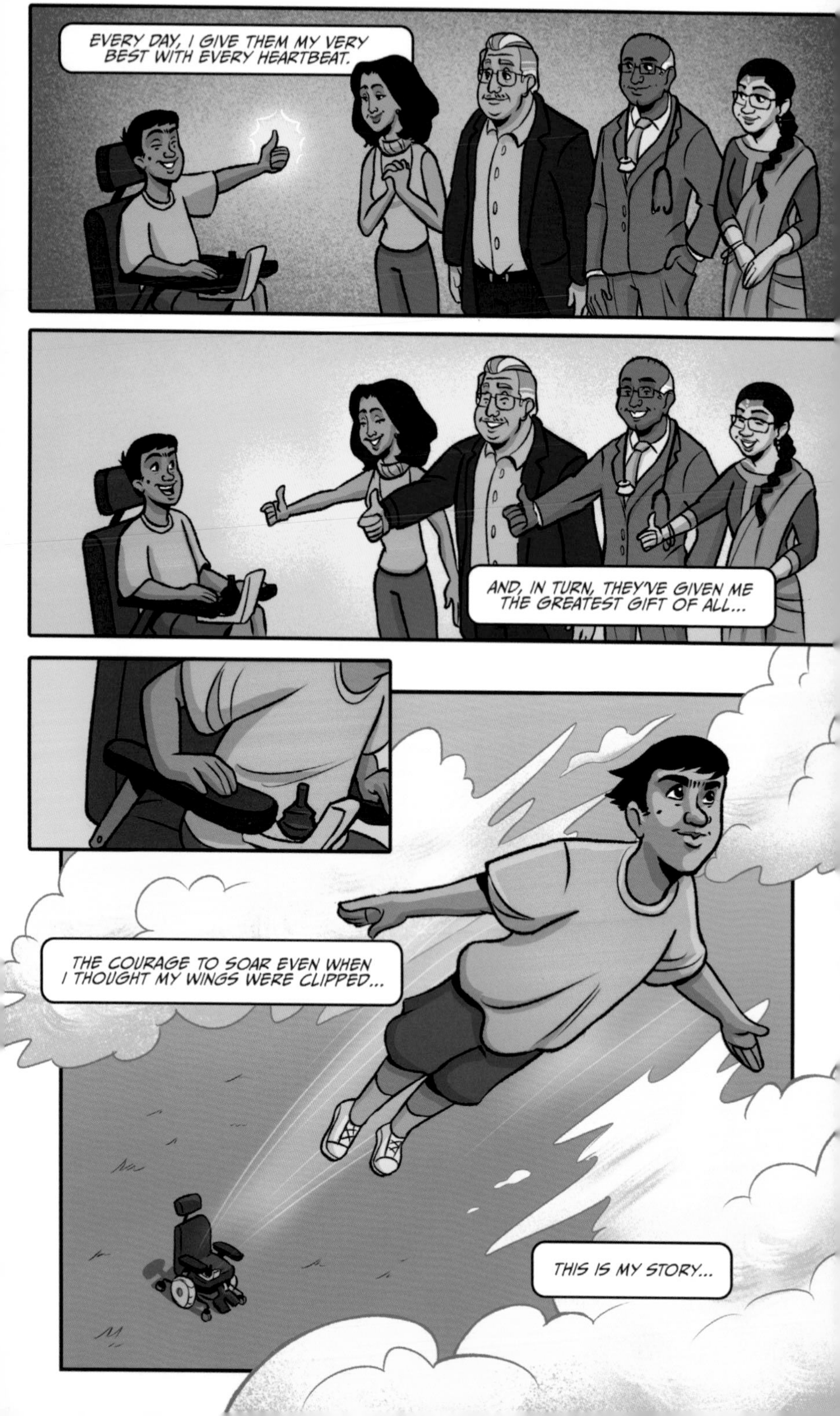
EVERY DAY, I GIVE THEM MY VERY BEST WITH EVERY HEARTBEAT.
AND, IN TURN, THEY'VE GIVEN ME THE GREATEST GIFT OF ALL...
THE COURAGE TO SOAR EVEN WHEN I THOUGHT MY WINGS WERE CLIPPED...
THIS IS MY STORY...

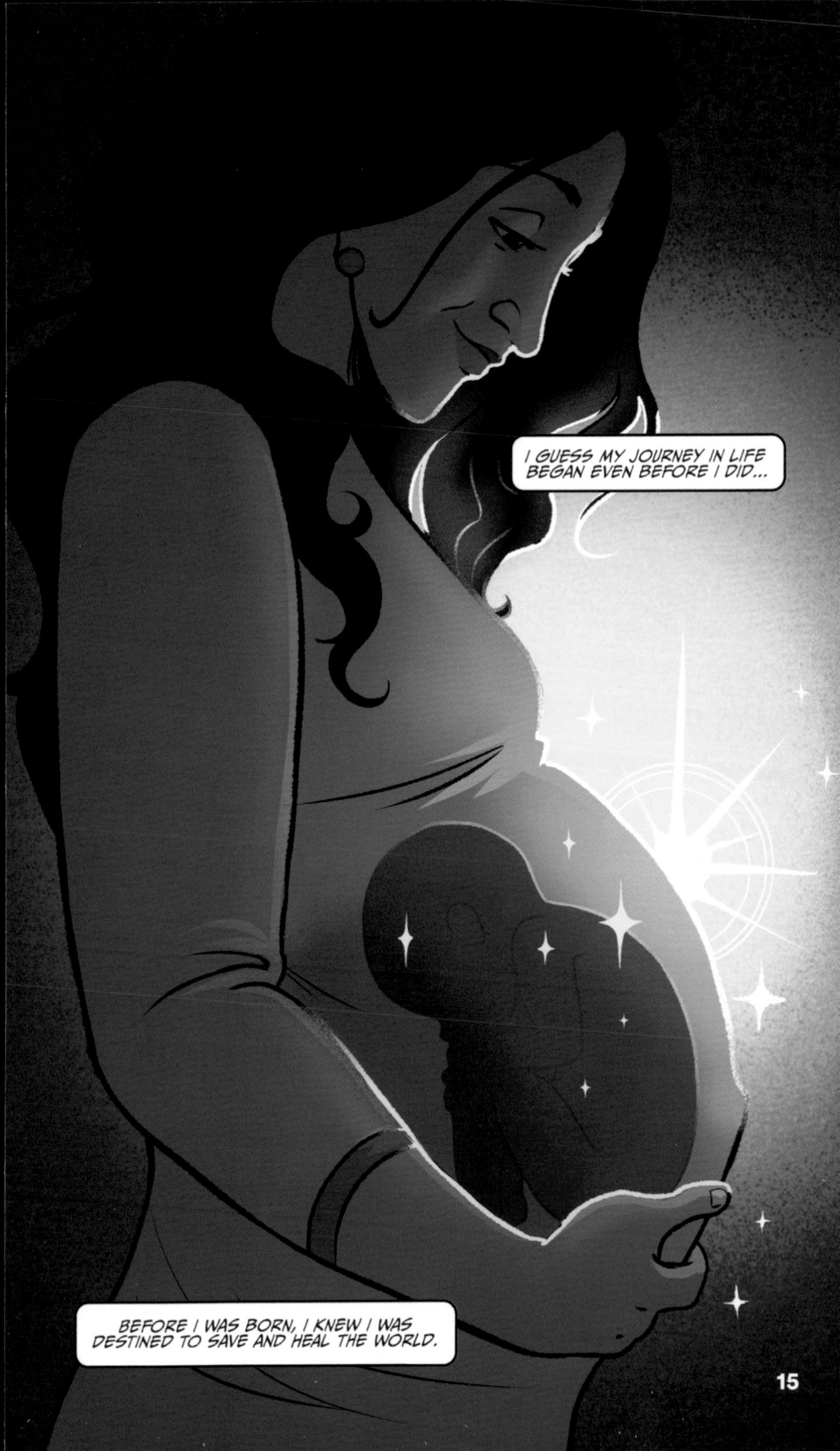
I GUESS MY JOURNEY IN LIFE BEGAN EVEN BEFORE I DID...
BEFORE I WAS BORN, I KNEW I WAS DESTINED TO SAVE AND HEAL THE WORLD.

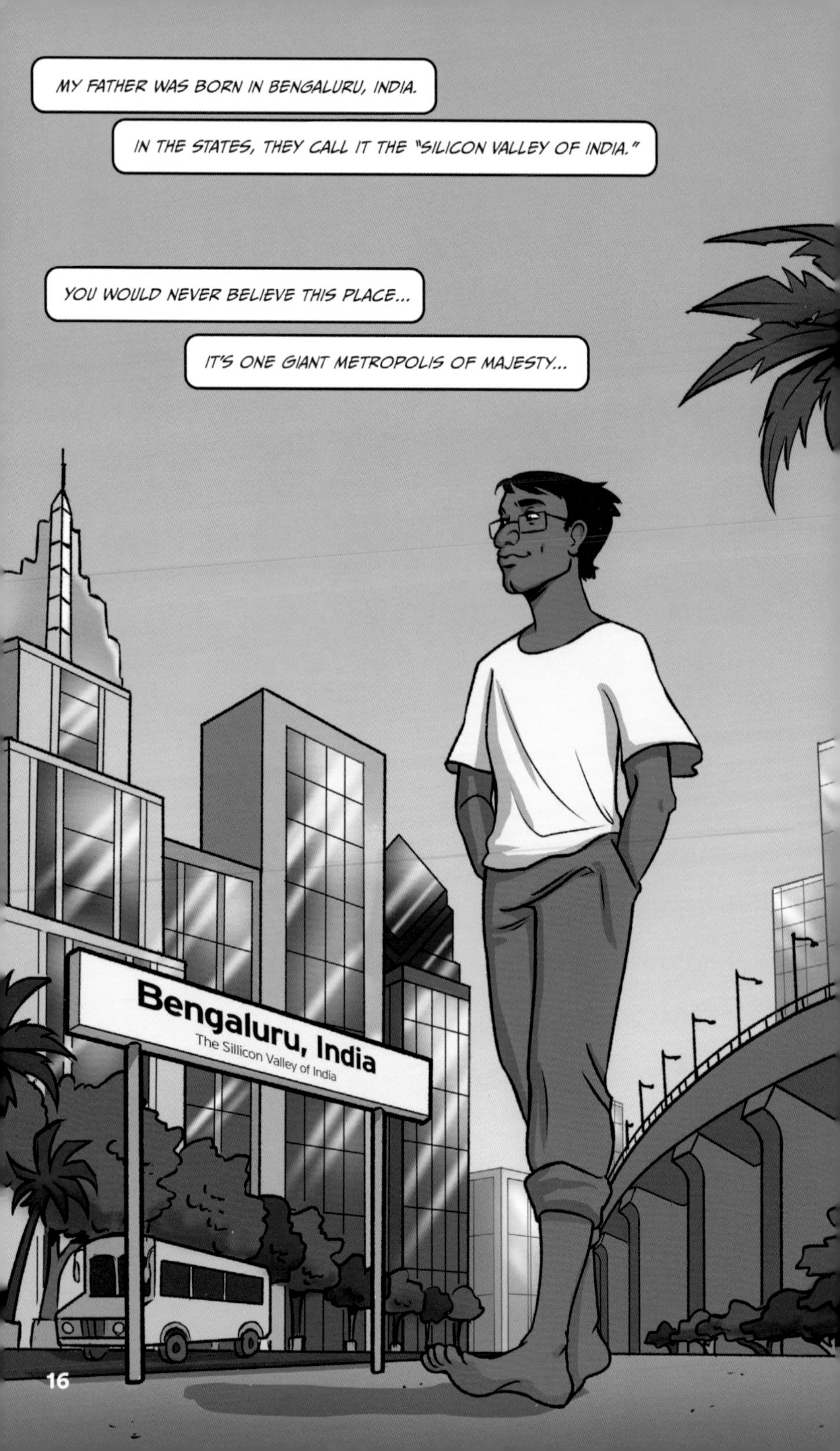
MY FATHER WAS BORN IN BENGALURU, INDIA.
IN THE STATES, THEY CALL IT THE "SILICON VALLEY OF INDIA."
YOU WOULD NEVER BELIEVE THIS PLACE...
IT'S ONE GIANT METROPOLIS OF MAJESTY...
Bengaluru, India
The Sillicon Valley of India

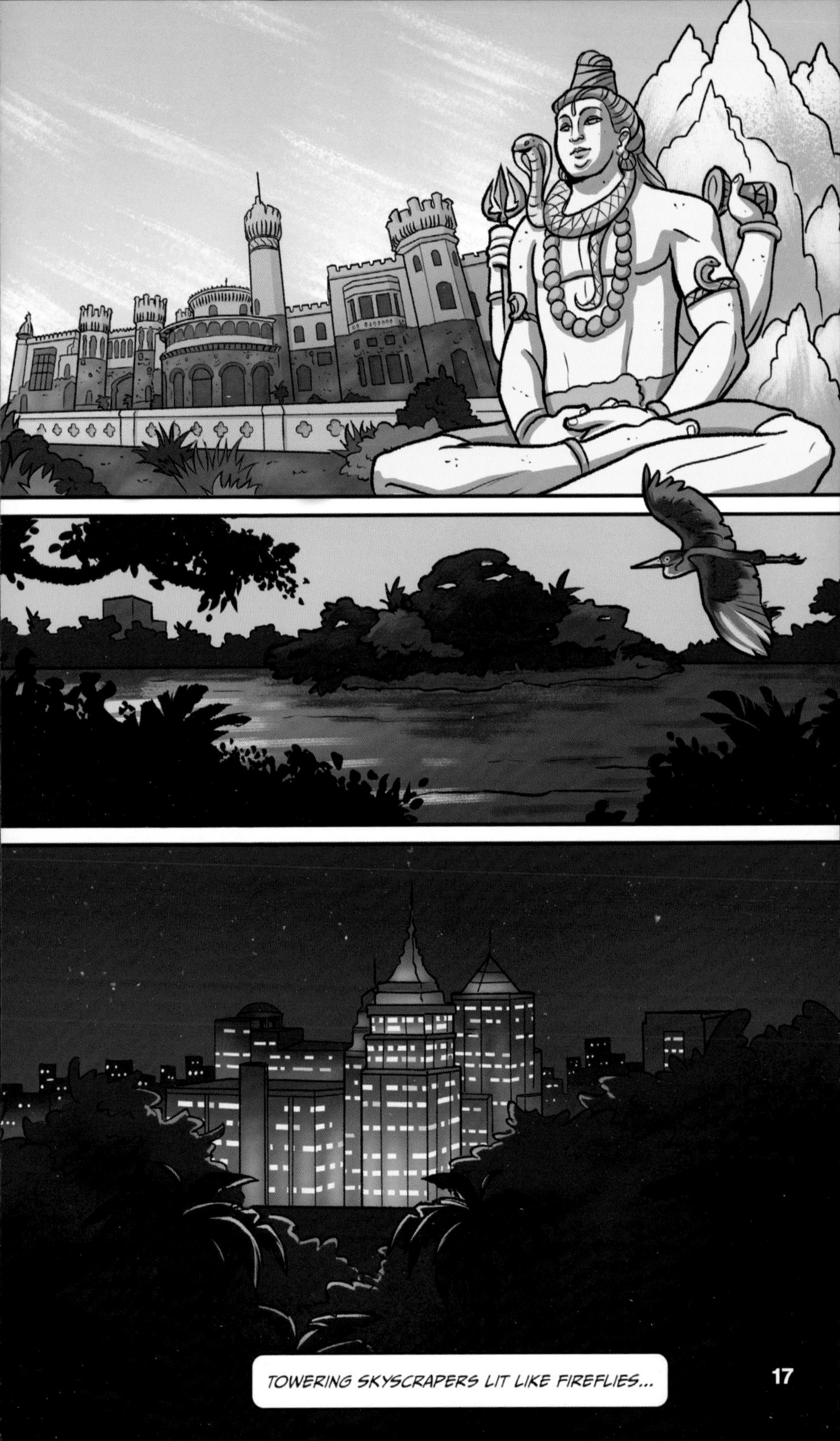
TOWERING SKYSCRAPERS LIT LIKE FIREFLIES...

A GLASS LADEN MULTI-MEDIA CENTER IN THE SHAPE OF A PYRAMID...

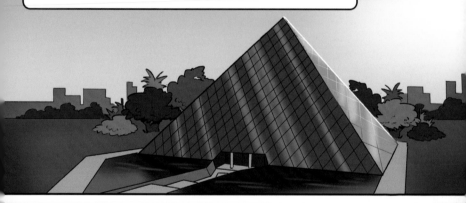

ARCHITECTONIC BUILDINGS THAT LOOK LIKE THEY FELL FROM THE FINGERTIPS OF BRAHMA...

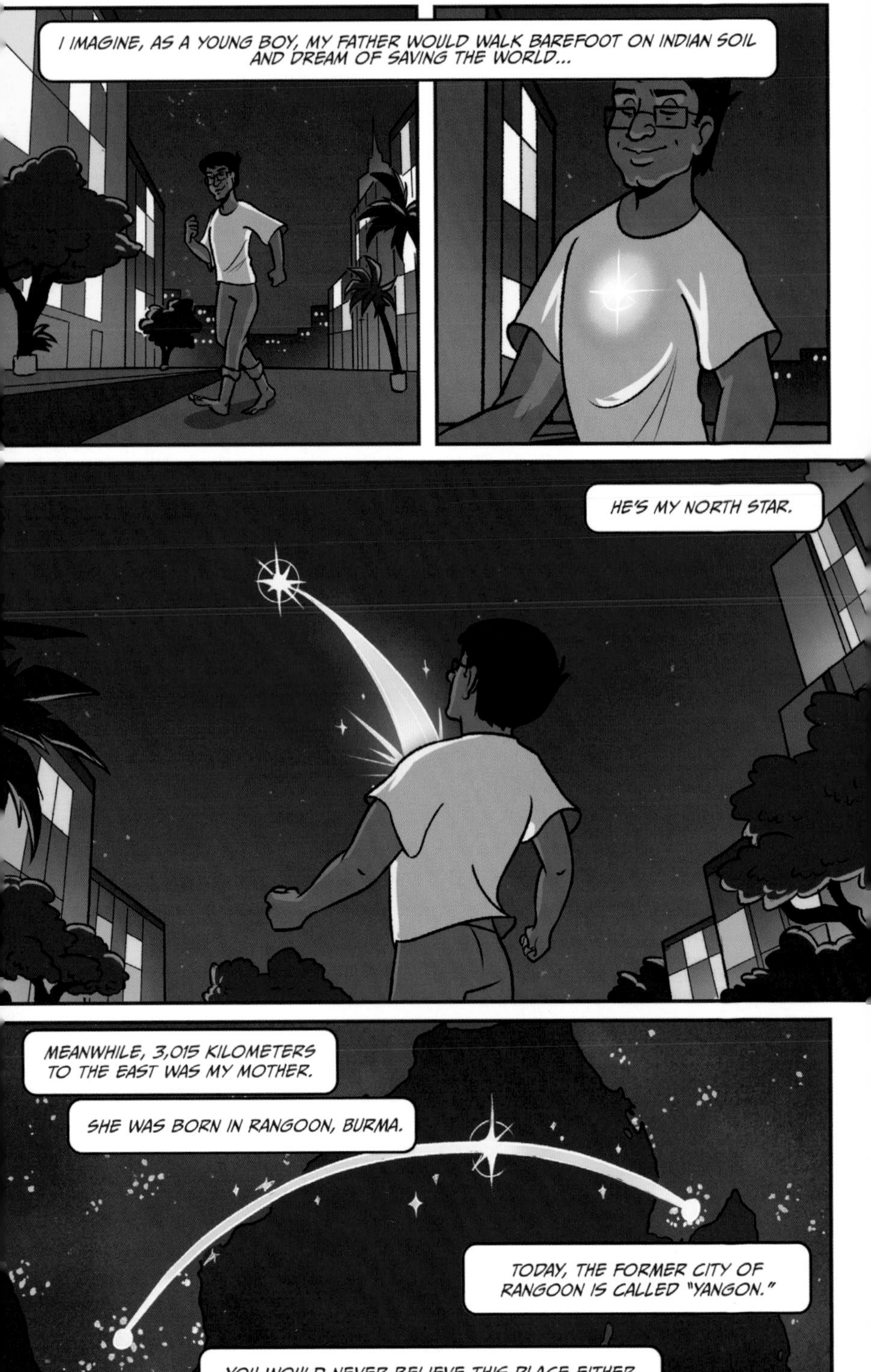
I IMAGINE, AS A YOUNG BOY, MY FATHER WOULD WALK BAREFOOT ON INDIAN SOIL AND DREAM OF SAVING THE WORLD...
HE'S MY NORTH STAR.
MEANWHILE, 3,015 KILOMETERS TO THE EAST WAS MY MOTHER.
SHE WAS BORN IN RANGOON, BURMA.
TODAY, THE FORMER CITY OF RANGOON IS CALLED "YANGON."
YOU WOULD NEVER BELIEVE THIS PLACE EITHER...

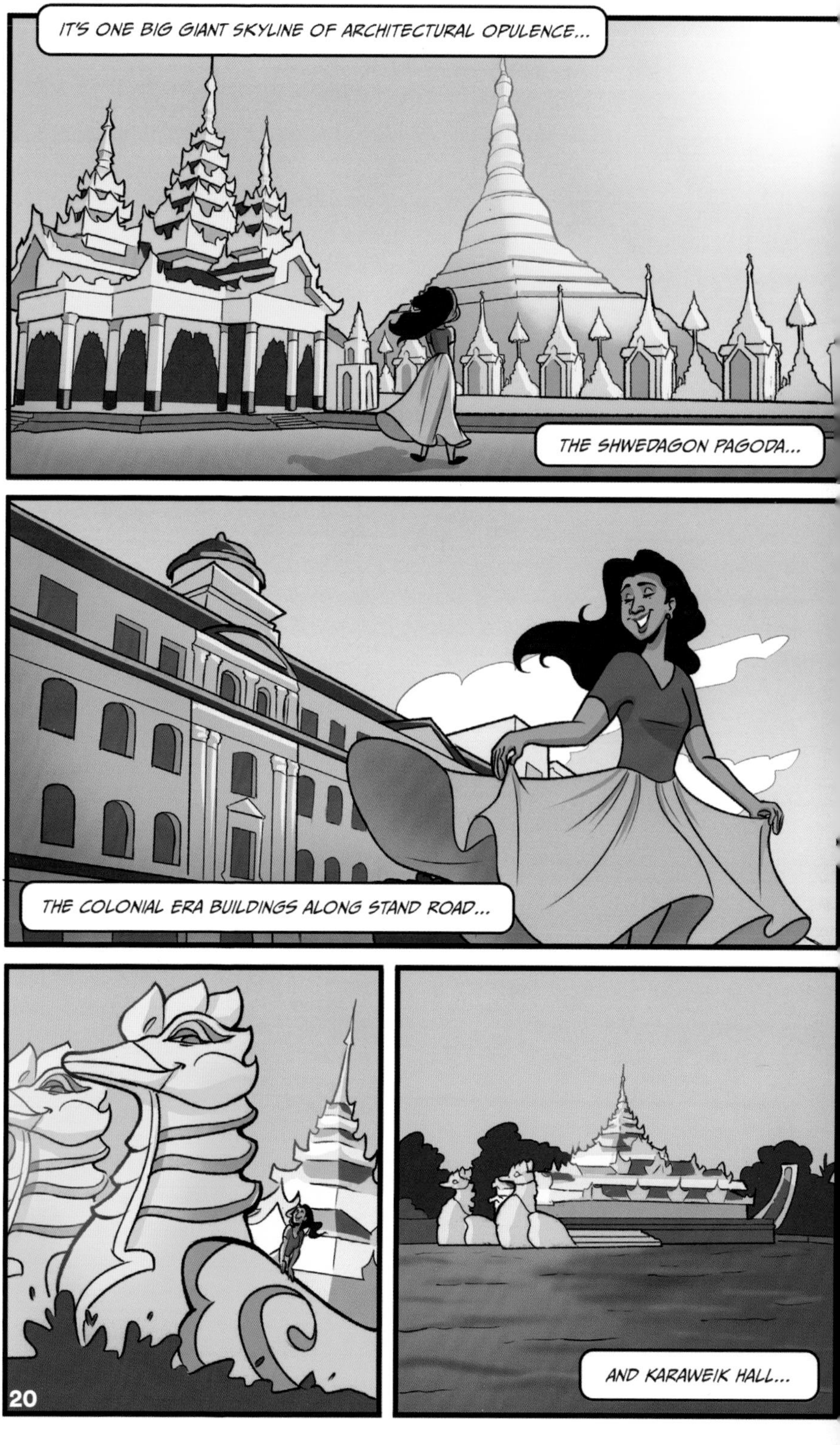
IT'S ONE BIG GIANT SKYLINE OF ARCHITECTURAL OPULENCE...
THE SHWEDAGON PAGODA...
THE COLONIAL ERA BUILDINGS ALONG STAND ROAD...
AND KARAWEIK HALL...

I IMAGINE MY MOTHER, AS A YOUNG GIRL, WOULD WALK BAREFOOT ON BURMESE SOIL AND DREAM OF HEALING THE WORLD...

WHO KNEW... 1873.434 MILES APART...

STOOD MY WHOLE SOUL... MY FATHER...

STOOD MY WHOLE HEART... MY MOTHER...

AND WHAT CAN BE MAPPED OUT AS A "PERFECT TRIANGLE" FROM INDIA TO BURMA TO AMERICA...

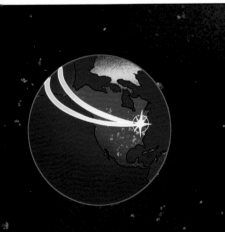

IT'S THE LATTER SIDE OF THE POLYGON WHERE MY JOURNEY TRULY BEGAN... WESTERN NEW YORK...

I WASN'T EVEN BORN YET, BUT FROM WHAT I HEARD...
MY MOTHER AND FATHER MET AT A COLLEGE PARTY...

ONE INTELLECTUAL CONVERSATION ABOUT SAVING
AND HEALING THE WORLD LED TO ANOTHER...

AND I WAS BORN... FEBRUARY 21, 1997.

FEBRUARY 1997

SUN	MON	TUE	WED	THU	FRI	SAT
						1
2	3	4	5	6	7	8
9	10	11	12	13	14	15
16	17	18	19	20	21	22
23	24	25	26	27	28	

TALK ABOUT KRISHNA.

MY MOTHER AND FATHER SENT OUT THE BIGGEST
AND BRIGHTEST BIRTH ANNOUNCEMENTS...

A Star
is Born
02.21.1997

"A STAR IS BORN..."

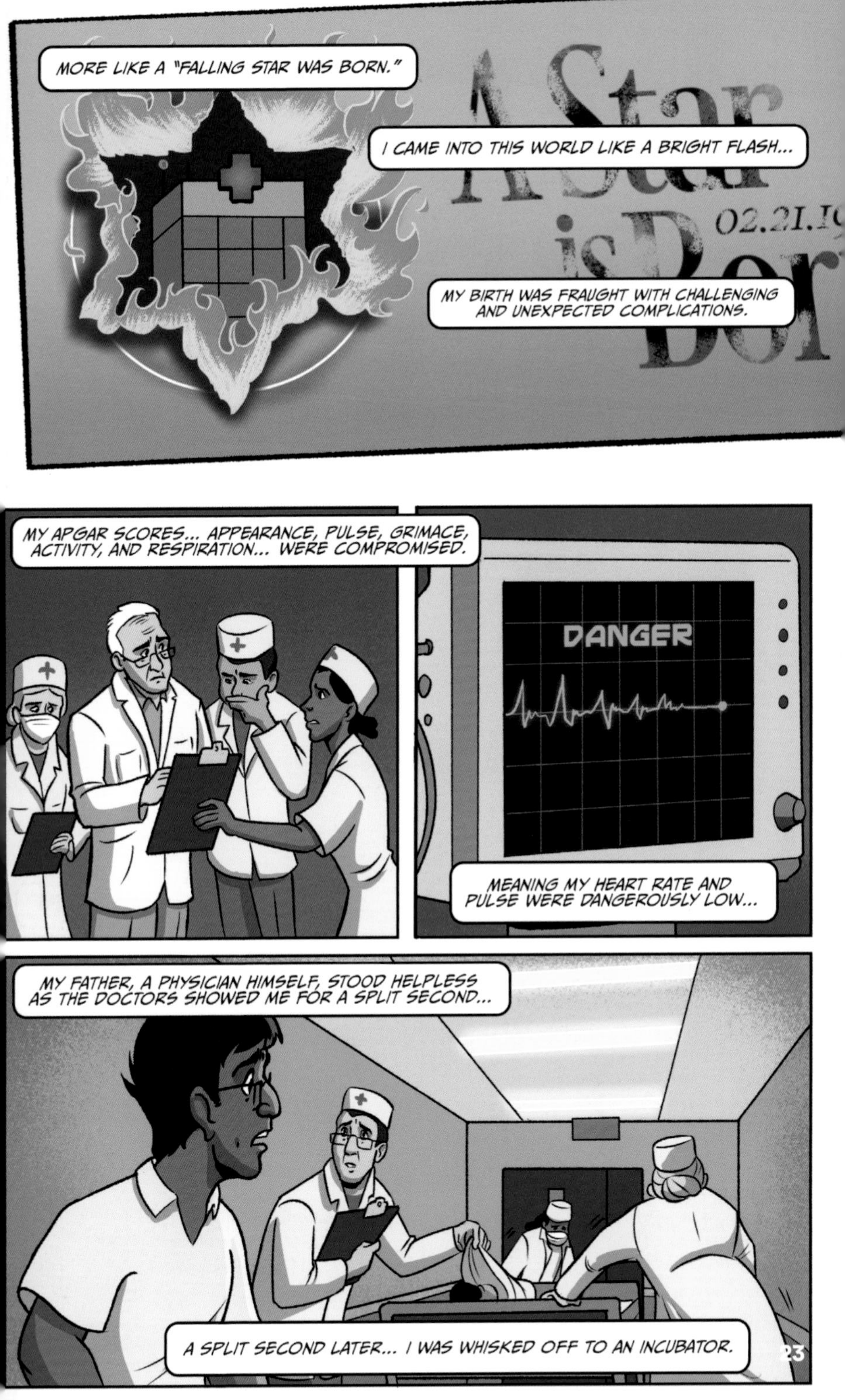
MORE LIKE A "FALLING STAR WAS BORN."
I CAME INTO THIS WORLD LIKE A BRIGHT FLASH...
MY BIRTH WAS FRAUGHT WITH CHALLENGING AND UNEXPECTED COMPLICATIONS.
MY APGAR SCORES... APPEARANCE, PULSE, GRIMACE, ACTIVITY, AND RESPIRATION... WERE COMPROMISED.
DANGER
MEANING MY HEART RATE AND PULSE WERE DANGEROUSLY LOW...
MY FATHER, A PHYSICIAN HIMSELF, STOOD HELPLESS AS THE DOCTORS SHOWED ME FOR A SPLIT SECOND...
A SPLIT SECOND LATER... I WAS WHISKED OFF TO AN INCUBATOR.

MUCH LIKE HOW A SHOOTING STAR...
GETS WHISKED AWAY INTO THE NIGHT SKYLINE...

I WAS SECONDS OLD.

I NEEDED TO BE RESUSCITATED...

I WAS BREATHING... BARELY...

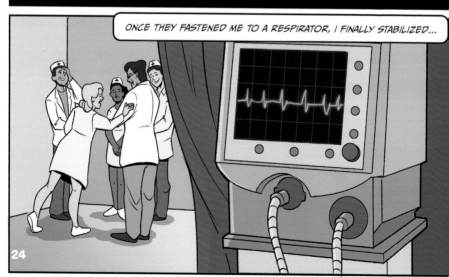

ONCE THEY FASTENED ME TO A RESPIRATOR, I FINALLY STABILIZED...

24

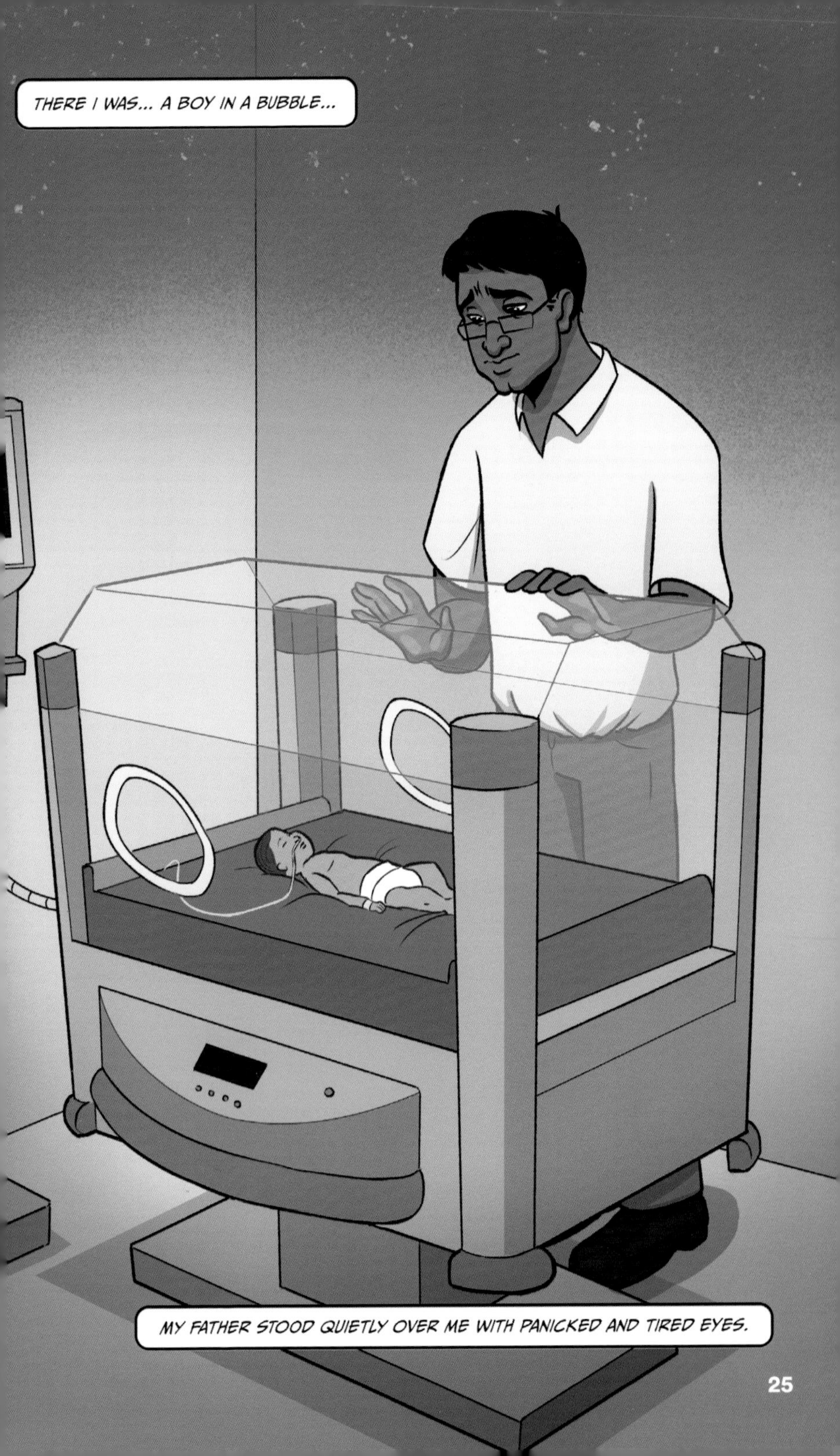
THERE I WAS... A BOY IN A BUBBLE...
MY FATHER STOOD QUIETLY OVER ME WITH PANICKED AND TIRED EYES.

HE SOFTLY EXCUSED HIMSELF AND WENT BACK TO CHECK ON MY MOTHER.

SHE QUIETLY ASKED...

HOW IS HE?

HE'S TINY...

FIVE POUNDS. SEVEN OUNCES. TO BE EXACT...

I WAS TWO POUNDS BELOW THE NATIONAL AVERAGE OF MALE BIRTHS...

Newborn Males
National Average

Michael	8 pounds 4 ounces
Jack	7 pounds 5 ounces
Benjamin	6 pounds 6 ounces
James	7 pounds 11 ounces
William	6 pounds 8 ounces
Elijah	7 pounds 3 ounces
Noah	8 pounds 2 ounces
Louis	6 pounds 11 ounces
David	7 pounds 9 ounces
Suneel	5 pounds 7 ounces

ONE IN 3,500 MALE BIRTHS ARE DIAGNOSED WITH DMD...

STATISTICALLY, I HAD MY WORK CUT OUT FOR ME...

ALTHOUGH I WAS ONLY HOURS OLD...

SOMEHOW I KNEW... I HAD TO LIVE UP TO MY NAME IF I WAS GOING TO SURVIVE.

AFTER ALL, I WAS NAMED AFTER A MAJOR DEITY IN HINDUISM.

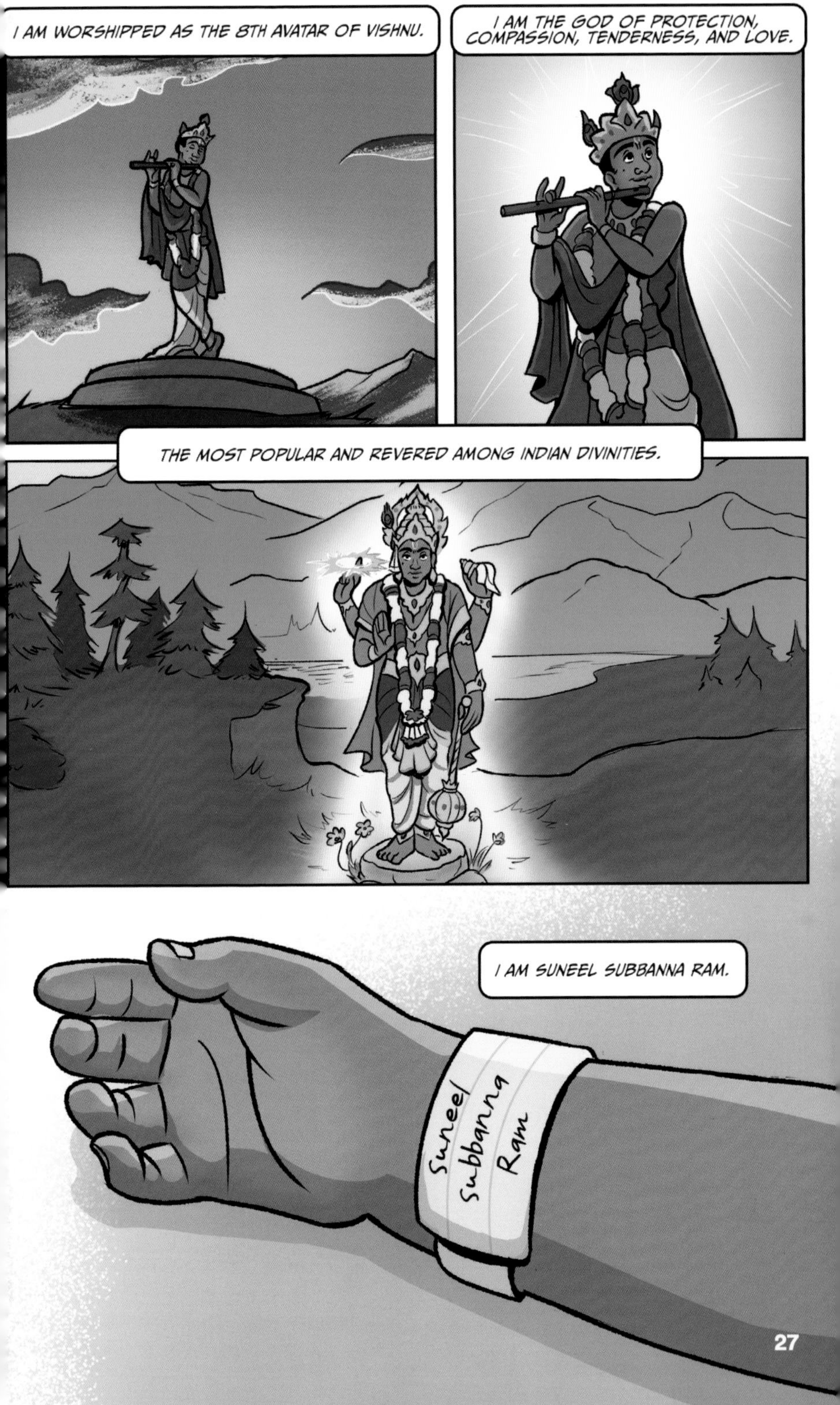
I AM WORSHIPPED AS THE 8TH AVATAR OF VISHNU.
I AM THE GOD OF PROTECTION, COMPASSION, TENDERNESS, AND LOVE.
THE MOST POPULAR AND REVERED AMONG INDIAN DIVINITIES.
I AM SUNEEL SUBBANNA RAM.
Suneel Subbanna Ram

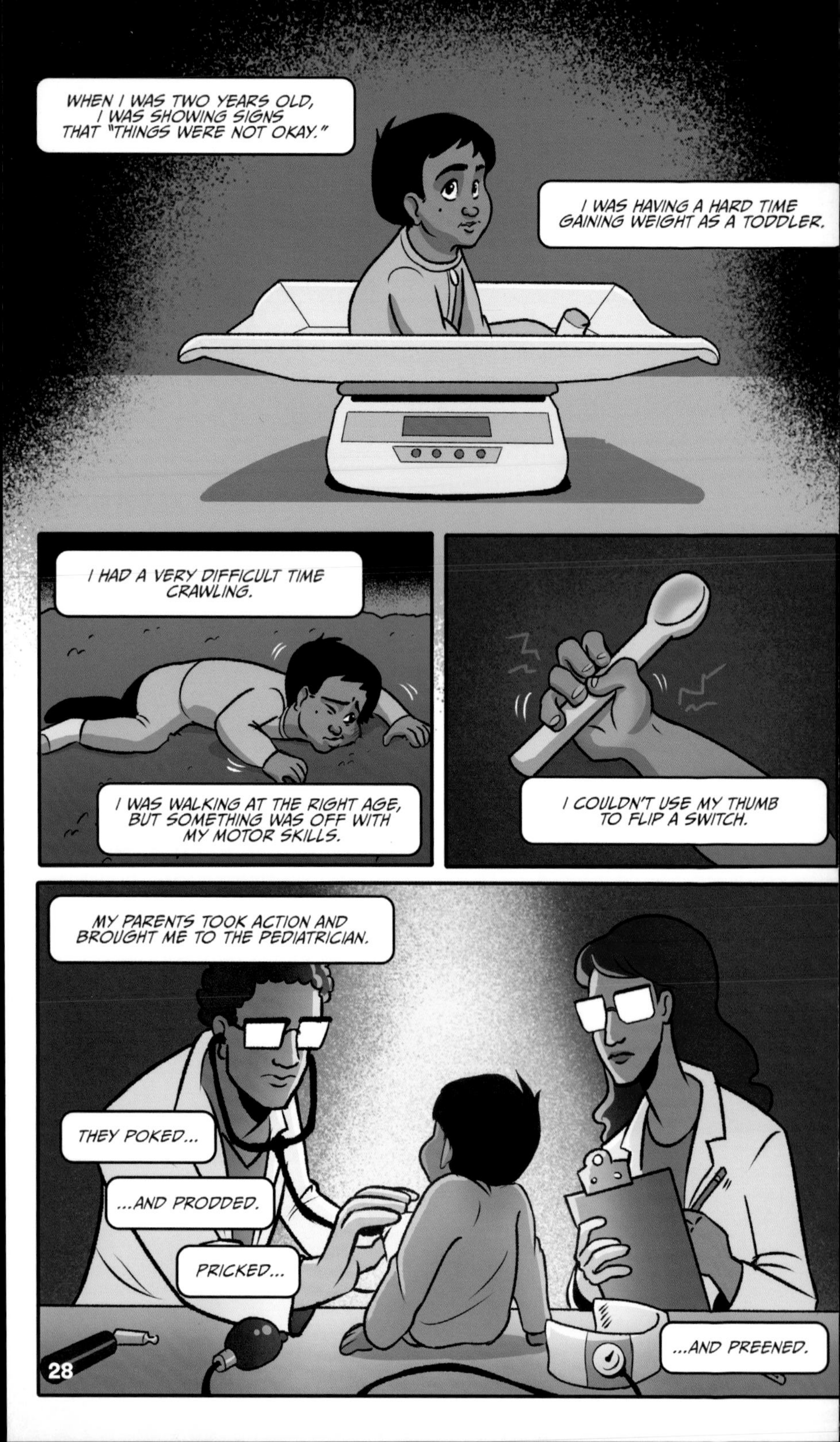

WHEN I WAS TWO YEARS OLD, I WAS SHOWING SIGNS THAT "THINGS WERE NOT OKAY."
I WAS HAVING A HARD TIME GAINING WEIGHT AS A TODDLER.
I HAD A VERY DIFFICULT TIME CRAWLING.
I WAS WALKING AT THE RIGHT AGE, BUT SOMETHING WAS OFF WITH MY MOTOR SKILLS.
I COULDN'T USE MY THUMB TO FLIP A SWITCH.
MY PARENTS TOOK ACTION AND BROUGHT ME TO THE PEDIATRICIAN.
THEY POKED...
...AND PRODDED.
PRICKED...
...AND PREENED.

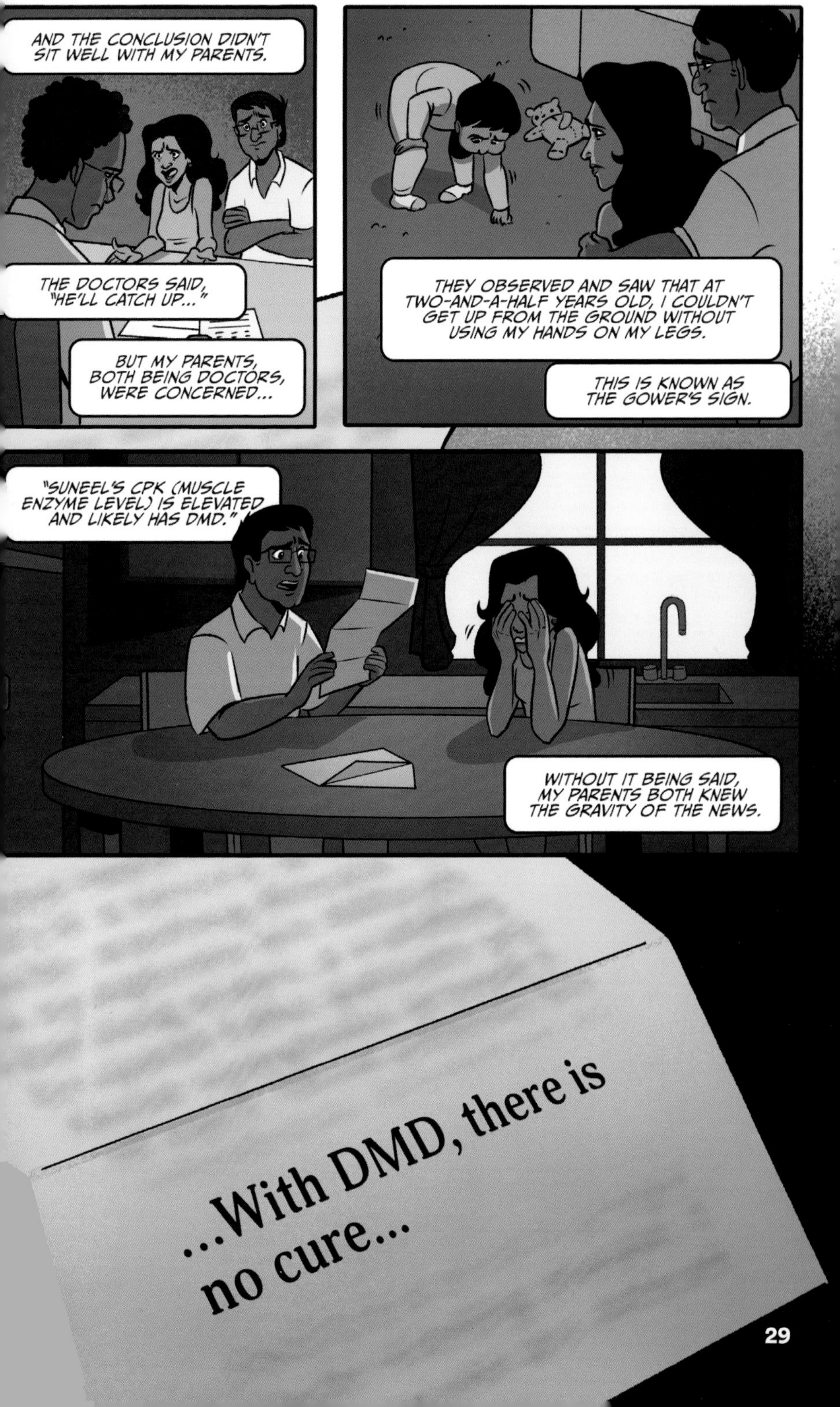
AND THE CONCLUSION DIDN'T SIT WELL WITH MY PARENTS.
THE DOCTORS SAID, "HE'LL CATCH UP..."
BUT MY PARENTS, BOTH BEING DOCTORS, WERE CONCERNED...
THEY OBSERVED AND SAW THAT AT TWO-AND-A-HALF YEARS OLD, I COULDN'T GET UP FROM THE GROUND WITHOUT USING MY HANDS ON MY LEGS.
THIS IS KNOWN AS THE GOWER'S SIGN.
"SUNEEL'S CPK (MUSCLE ENZYME LEVEL) IS ELEVATED AND LIKELY HAS DMD."
WITHOUT IT BEING SAID, MY PARENTS BOTH KNEW THE GRAVITY OF THE NEWS.
...With DMD, there is no cure...

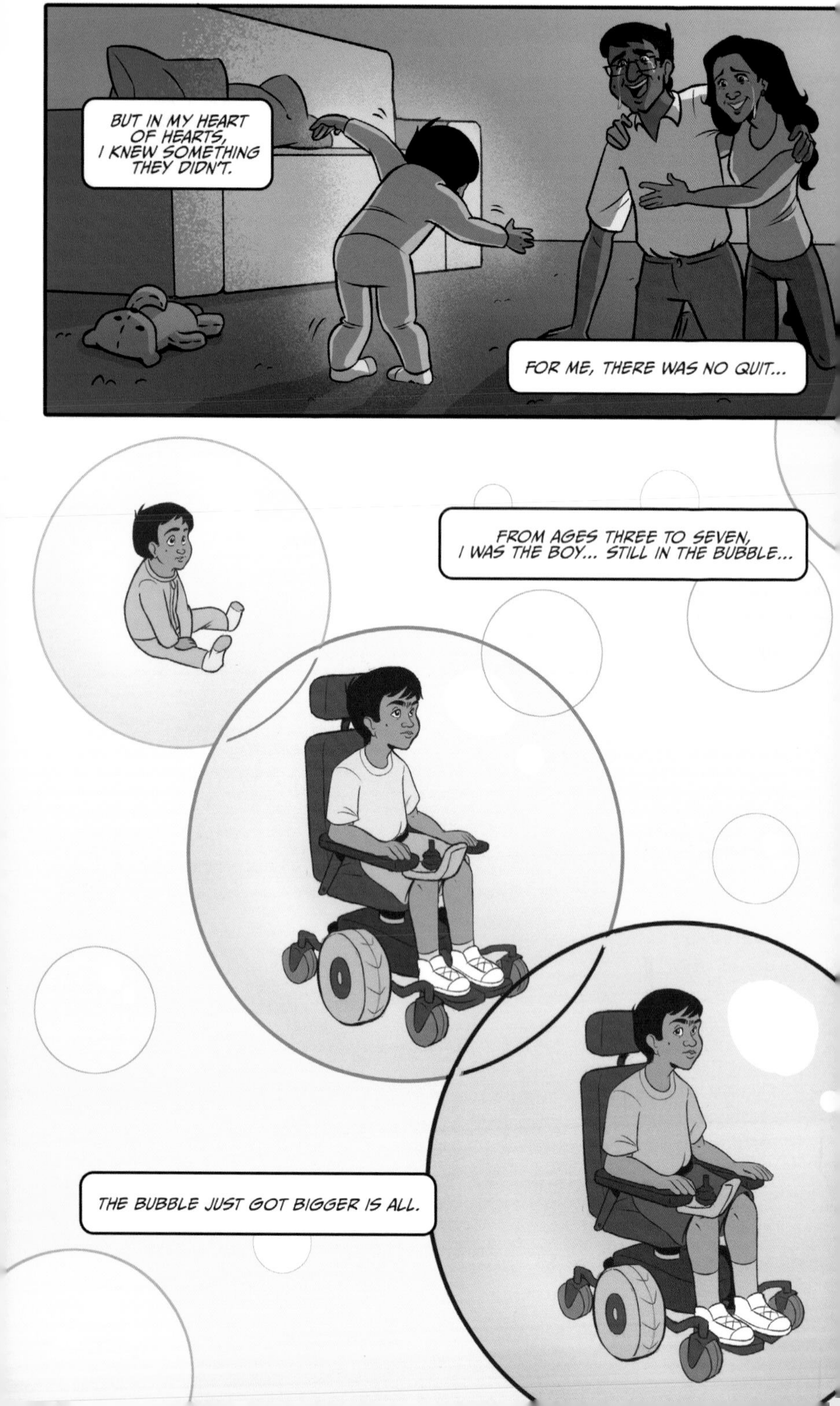
BUT IN MY HEART OF HEARTS, I KNEW SOMETHING THEY DIDN'T.
FOR ME, THERE WAS NO QUIT...
FROM AGES THREE TO SEVEN, I WAS THE BOY... STILL IN THE BUBBLE...
THE BUBBLE JUST GOT BIGGER IS ALL.

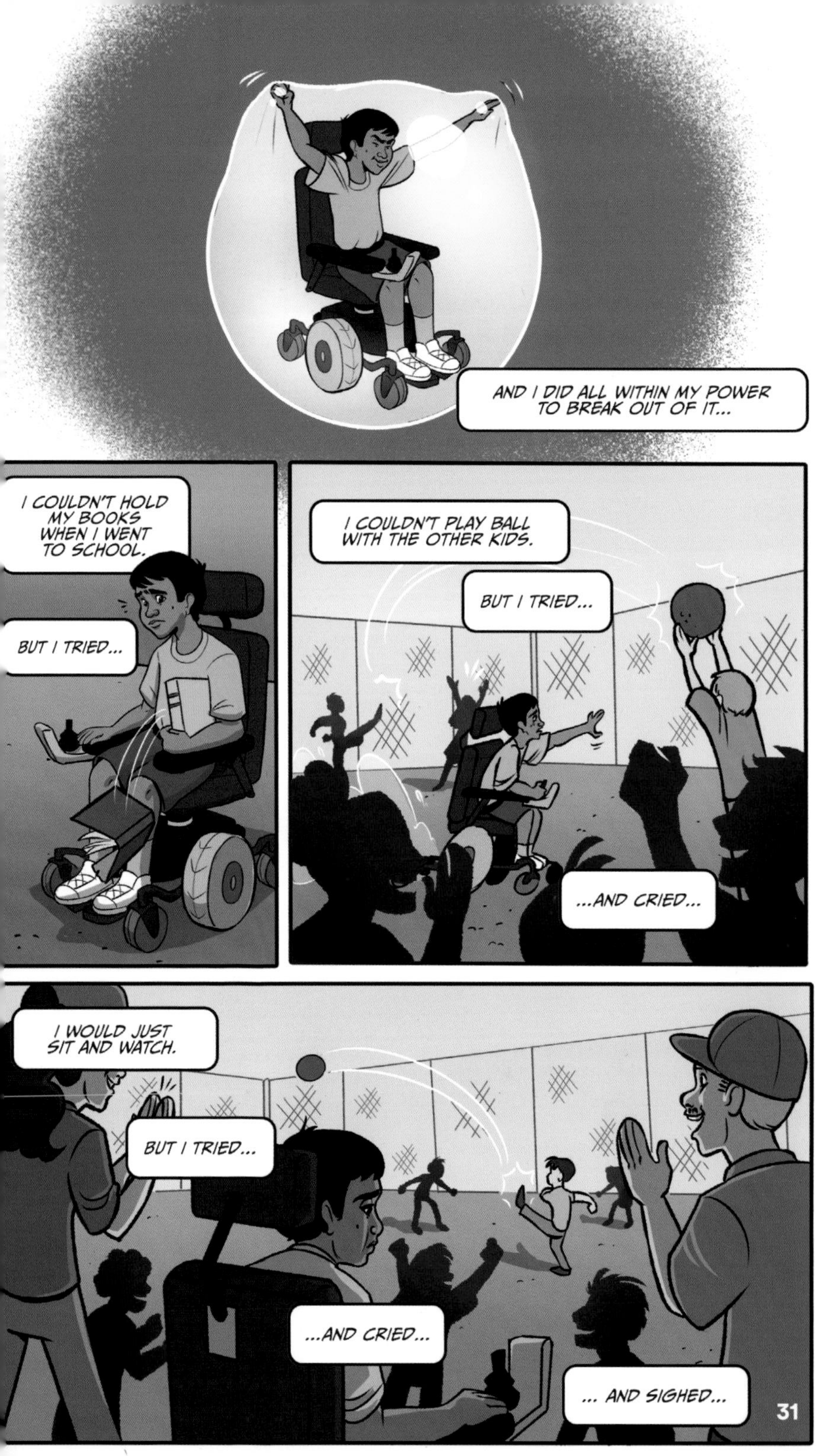
AND I DID ALL WITHIN MY POWER TO BREAK OUT OF IT...
I COULDN'T HOLD MY BOOKS WHEN I WENT TO SCHOOL.
BUT I TRIED...
I COULDN'T PLAY BALL WITH THE OTHER KIDS.
BUT I TRIED...
...AND CRIED...
I WOULD JUST SIT AND WATCH.
BUT I TRIED...
...AND CRIED...
... AND SIGHED...

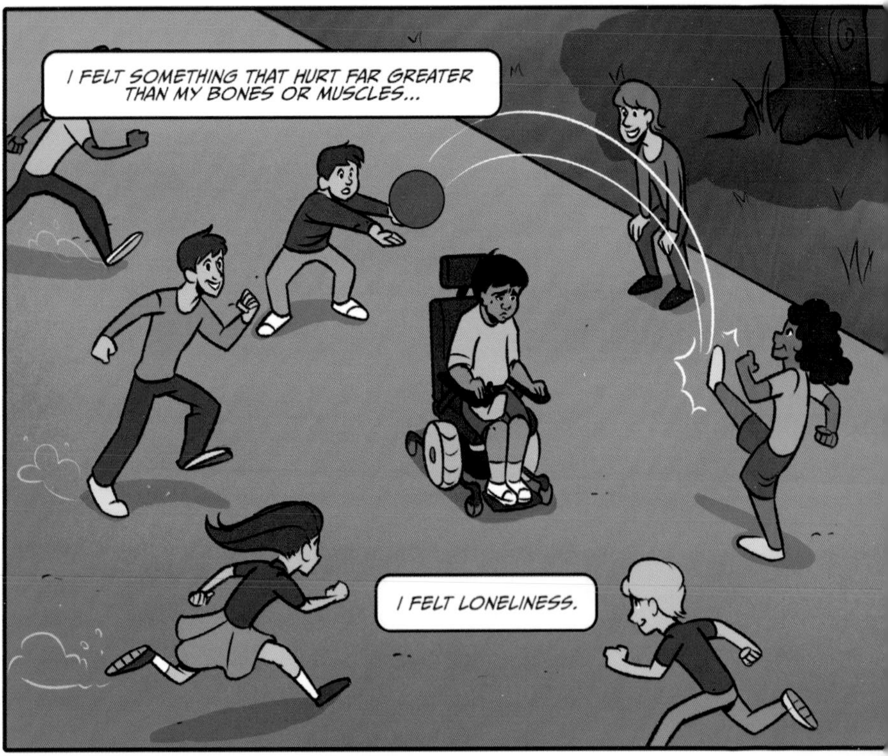
I FELT SOMETHING THAT HURT FAR GREATER THAN MY BONES OR MUSCLES...
I FELT LONELINESS.

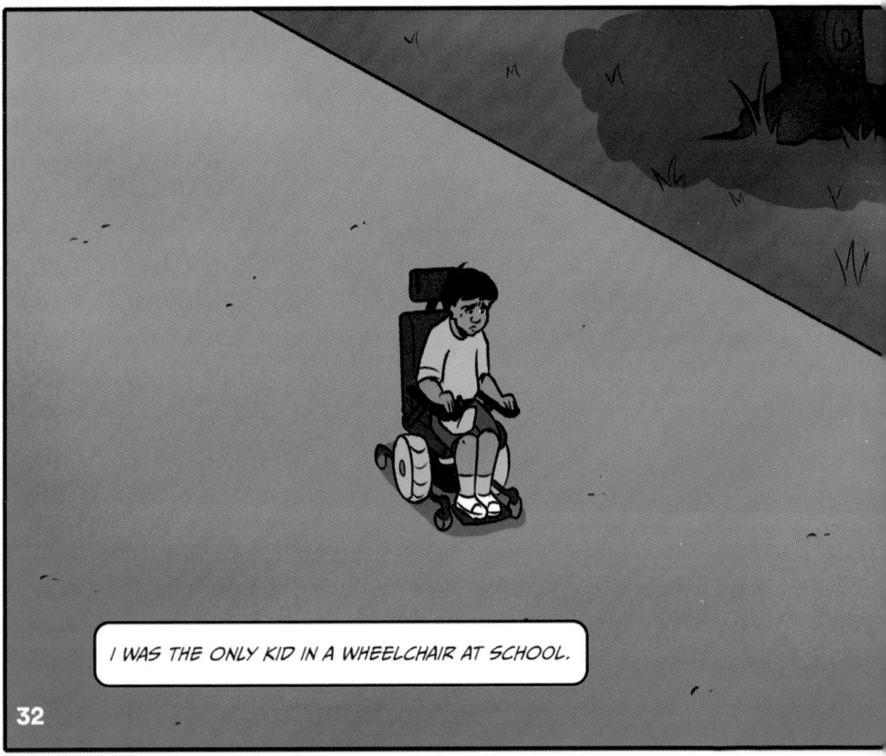
I WAS THE ONLY KID IN A WHEELCHAIR AT SCHOOL.

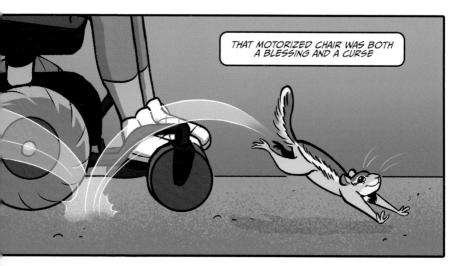

THAT MOTORIZED CHAIR WAS BOTH A BLESSING AND A CURSE

IT'S A "BLESSING" BECAUSE IT HELPED ME SAVE MY STRENGTH...

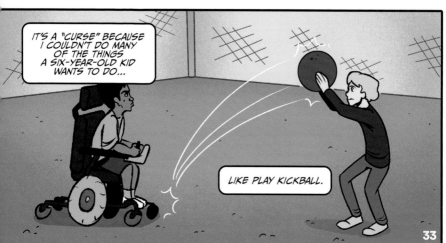

IT'S A "CURSE" BECAUSE I COULDN'T DO MANY OF THE THINGS A SIX-YEAR-OLD KID WANTS TO DO...

LIKE PLAY KICKBALL.

I'D JUST WATCH QUIETLY FROM THE SIDELINES WITH A NOVOCAIN SMILE ON MY FACE.
AFTER A WHILE, MY SMILE WOULD SIMPLY WEAR OFF...

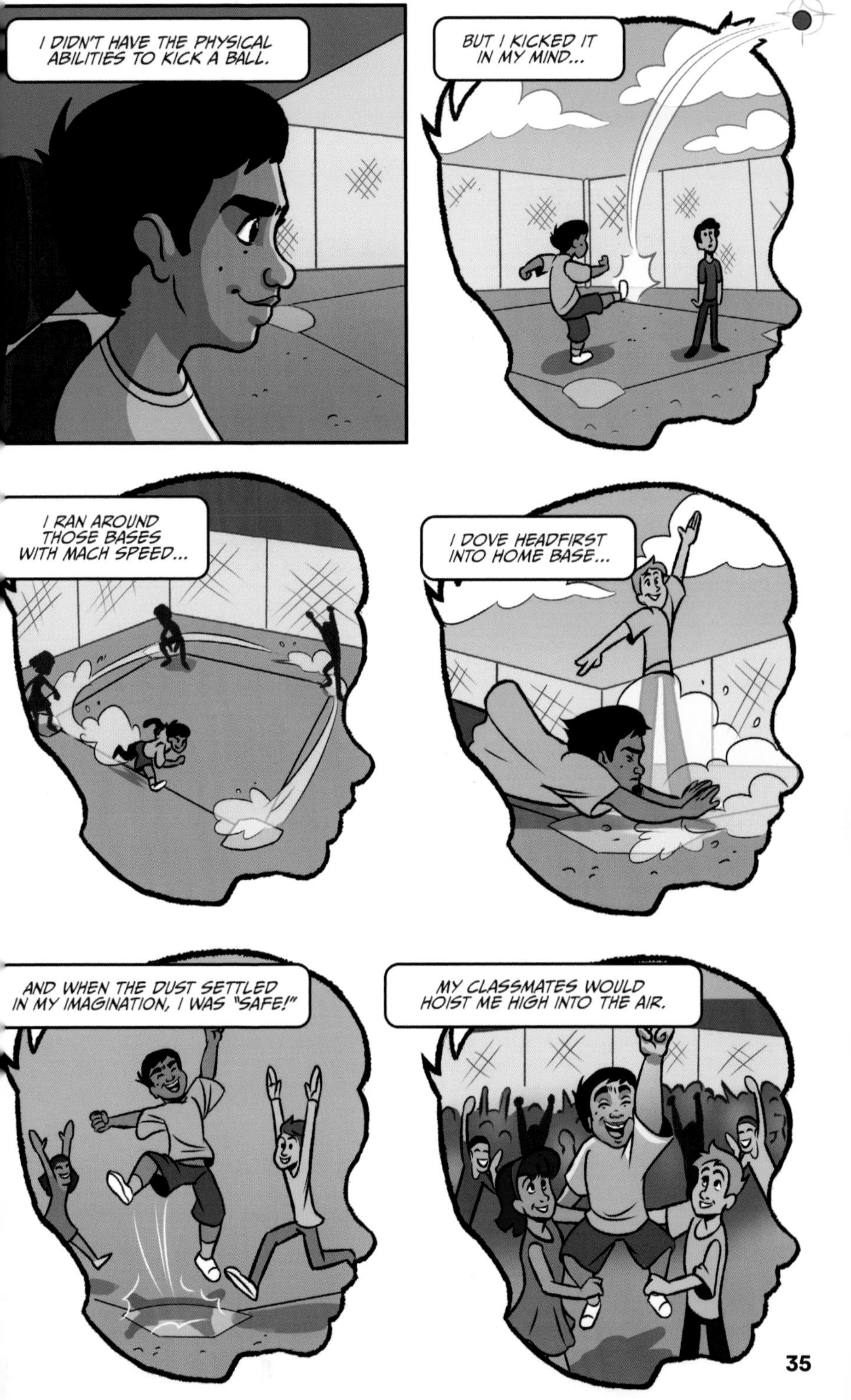
I DIDN'T HAVE THE PHYSICAL ABILITIES TO KICK A BALL.
BUT I KICKED IT IN MY MIND...
I RAN AROUND THOSE BASES WITH MACH SPEED...
I DOVE HEADFIRST INTO HOME BASE...
AND WHEN THE DUST SETTLED IN MY IMAGINATION, I WAS "SAFE!"
MY CLASSMATES WOULD HOIST ME HIGH INTO THE AIR.

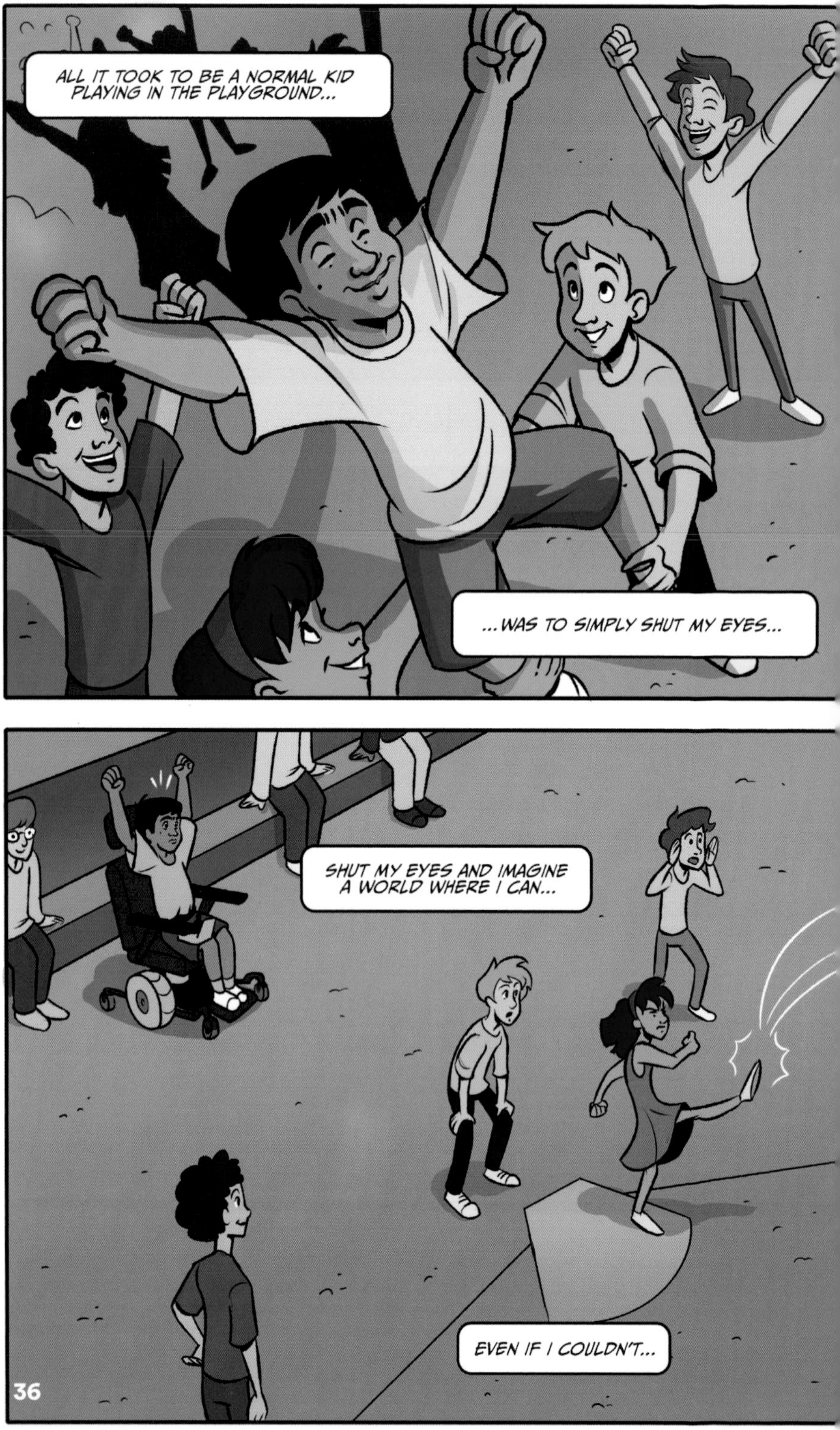
ALL IT TOOK TO BE A NORMAL KID PLAYING IN THE PLAYGROUND...
...WAS TO SIMPLY SHUT MY EYES...
SHUT MY EYES AND IMAGINE A WORLD WHERE I CAN...
EVEN IF I COULDN'T...

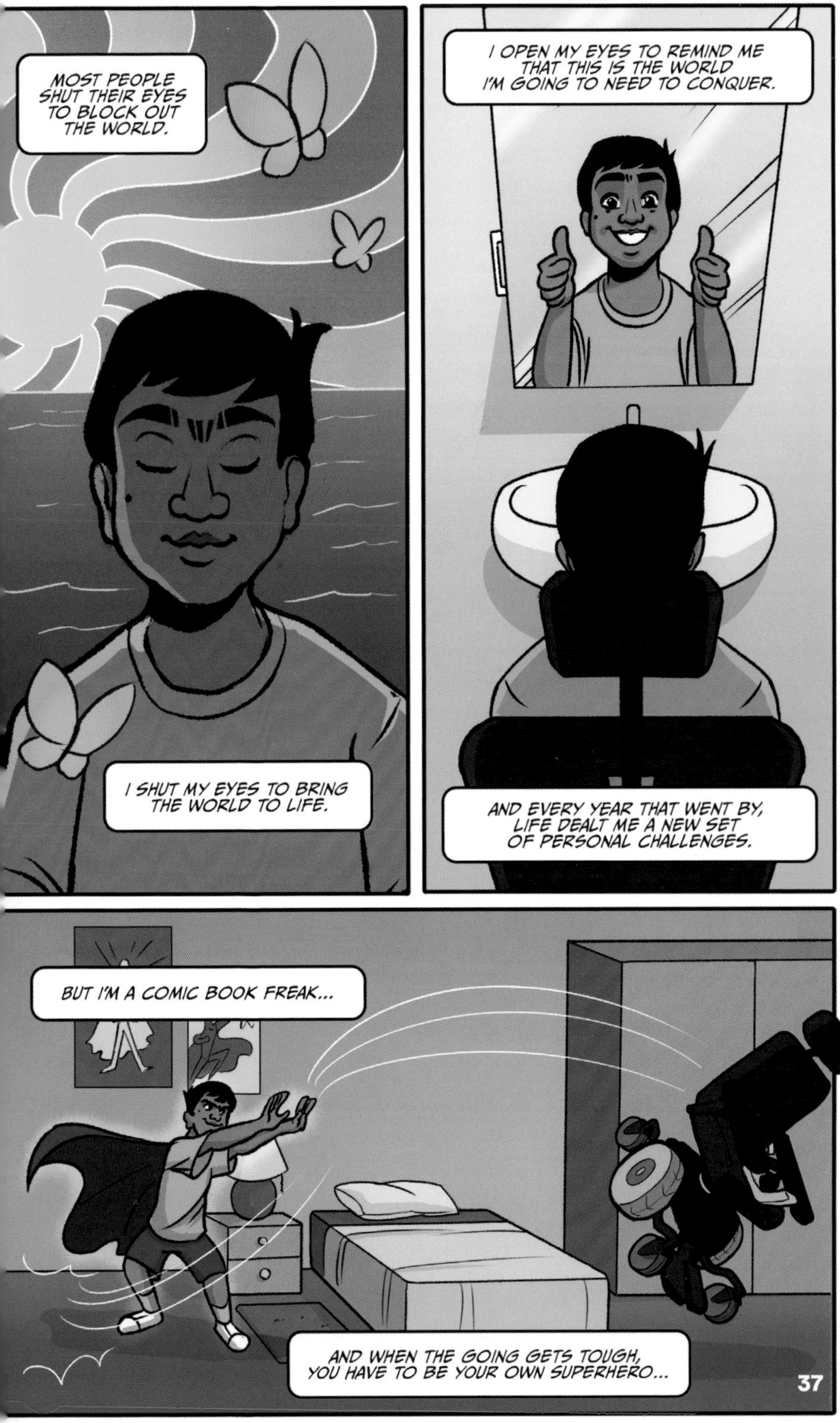

MOST PEOPLE SHUT THEIR EYES TO BLOCK OUT THE WORLD.
I SHUT MY EYES TO BRING THE WORLD TO LIFE.
I OPEN MY EYES TO REMIND ME THAT THIS IS THE WORLD I'M GOING TO NEED TO CONQUER.
AND EVERY YEAR THAT WENT BY, LIFE DEALT ME A NEW SET OF PERSONAL CHALLENGES.
BUT I'M A COMIC BOOK FREAK...
AND WHEN THE GOING GETS TOUGH, YOU HAVE TO BE YOUR OWN SUPERHERO...

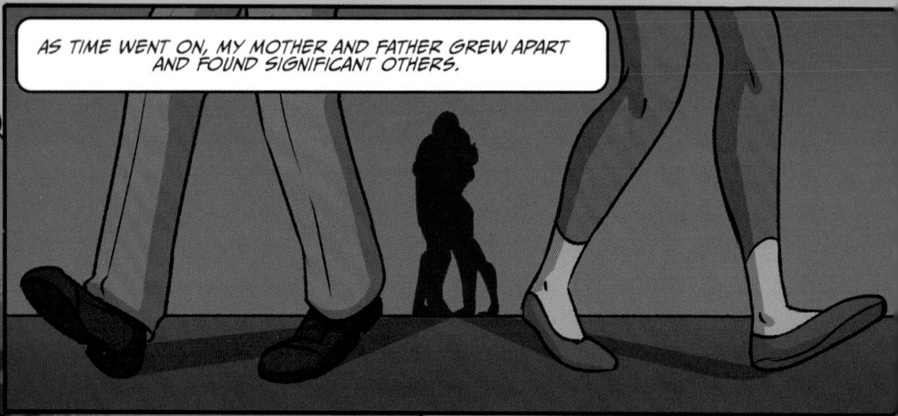
AS TIME WENT ON, MY MOTHER AND FATHER GREW APART AND FOUND SIGNIFICANT OTHERS.

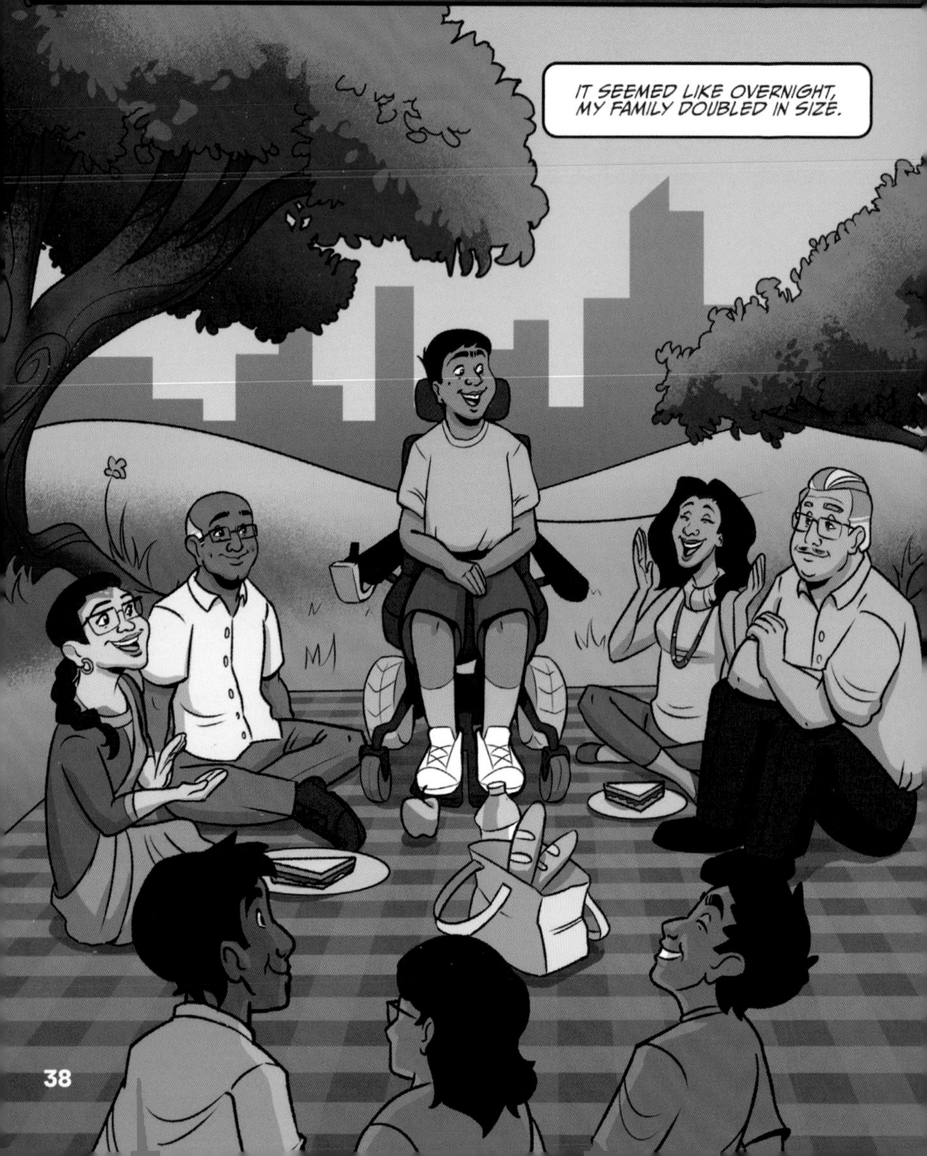
IT SEEMED LIKE OVERNIGHT, MY FAMILY DOUBLED IN SIZE.

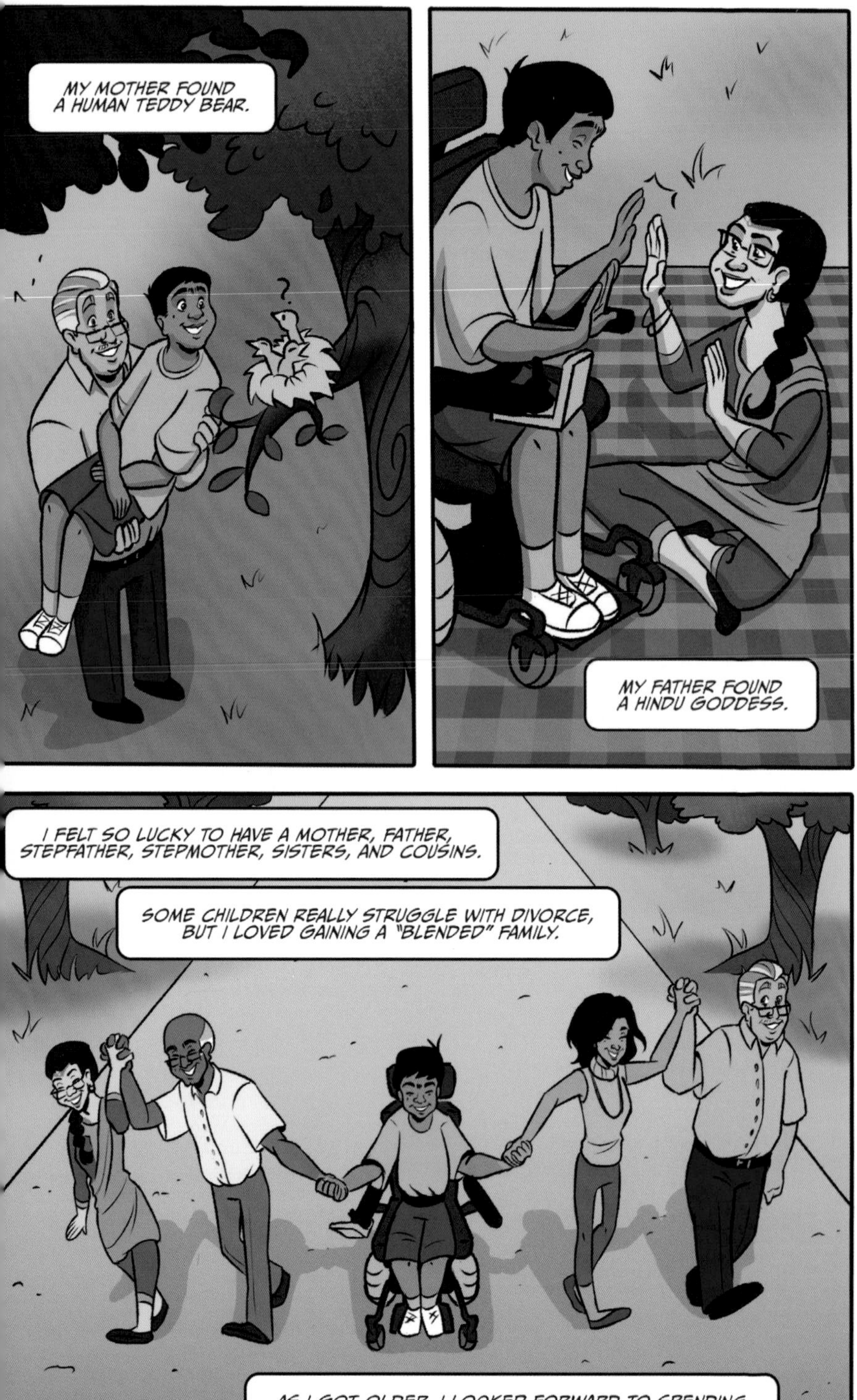
MY MOTHER FOUND A HUMAN TEDDY BEAR.
?
MY FATHER FOUND A HINDU GODDESS.
I FELT SO LUCKY TO HAVE A MOTHER, FATHER, STEPFATHER, STEPMOTHER, SISTERS, AND COUSINS.
SOME CHILDREN REALLY STRUGGLE WITH DIVORCE, BUT I LOVED GAINING A "BLENDED" FAMILY.
AS I GOT OLDER, I LOOKED FORWARD TO SPENDING "ONE-ON-ONE" TIME WITH THE ONES THAT I LOVE

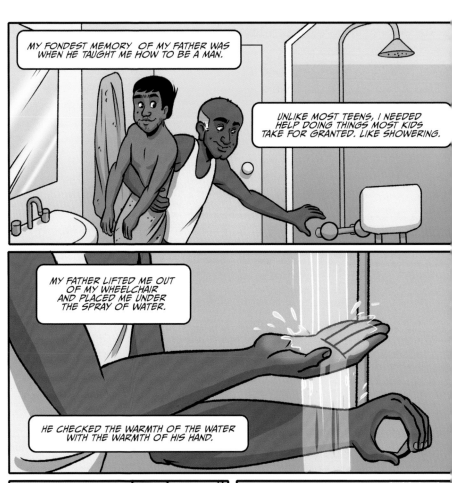

MY FONDEST MEMORY OF MY FATHER WAS WHEN HE TAUGHT ME HOW TO BE A MAN.

UNLIKE MOST TEENS, I NEEDED HELP DOING THINGS MOST KIDS TAKE FOR GRANTED. LIKE SHOWERING.

MY FATHER LIFTED ME OUT OF MY WHEELCHAIR AND PLACED ME UNDER THE SPRAY OF WATER.

HE CHECKED THE WARMTH OF THE WATER WITH THE WARMTH OF HIS HAND.

HE'D HELP ME WASH MY UPPER BODY...

AND LATHER SOAP ON THE TOP OF MY HEAD.

40

I ALWAYS FELT BAD BECAUSE HE'D BE MORE SOAKED THAN I WAS.

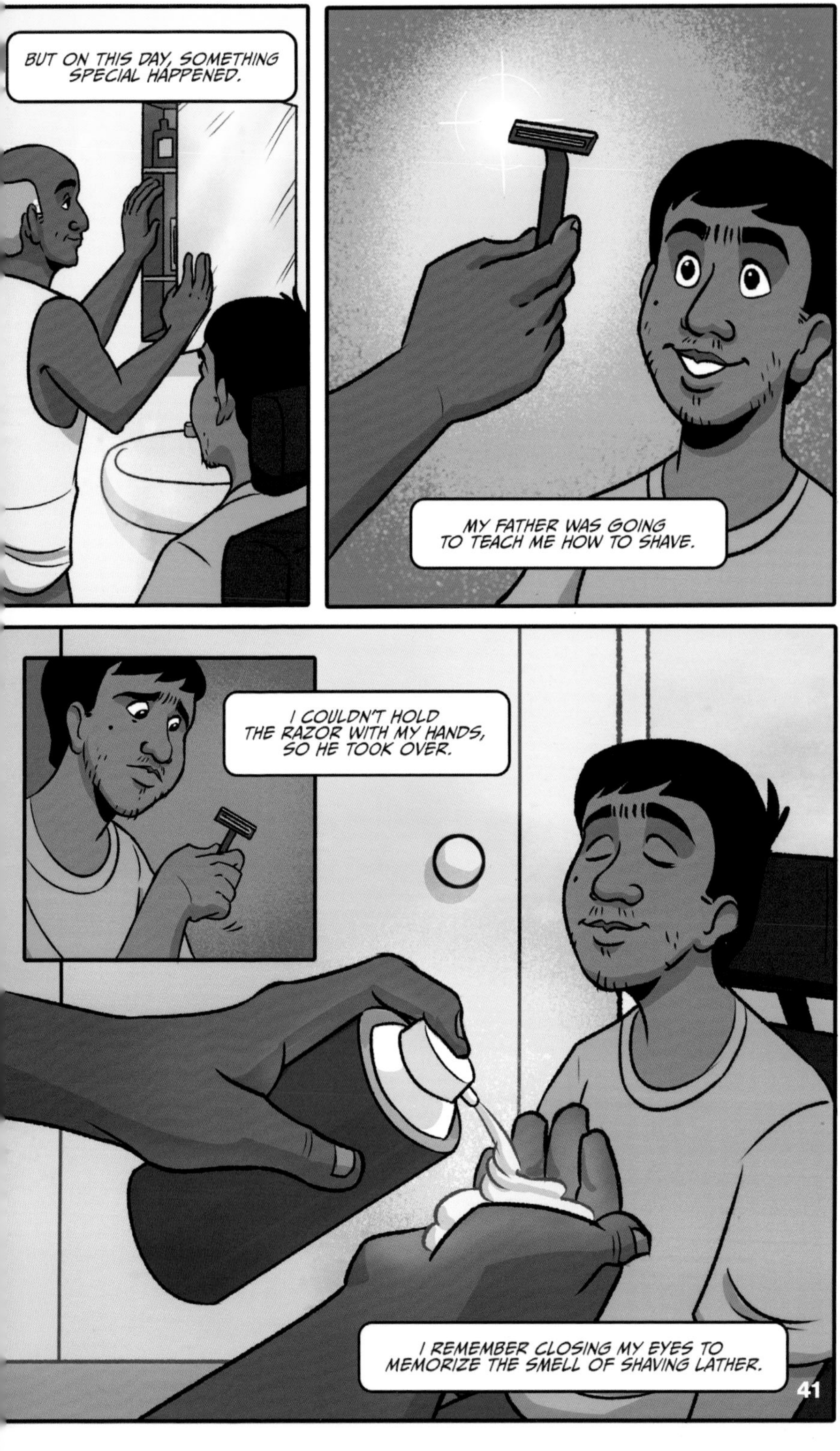
BUT ON THIS DAY, SOMETHING SPECIAL HAPPENED.
MY FATHER WAS GOING TO TEACH ME HOW TO SHAVE.
I COULDN'T HOLD THE RAZOR WITH MY HANDS, SO HE TOOK OVER.
I REMEMBER CLOSING MY EYES TO MEMORIZE THE SMELL OF SHAVING LATHER.

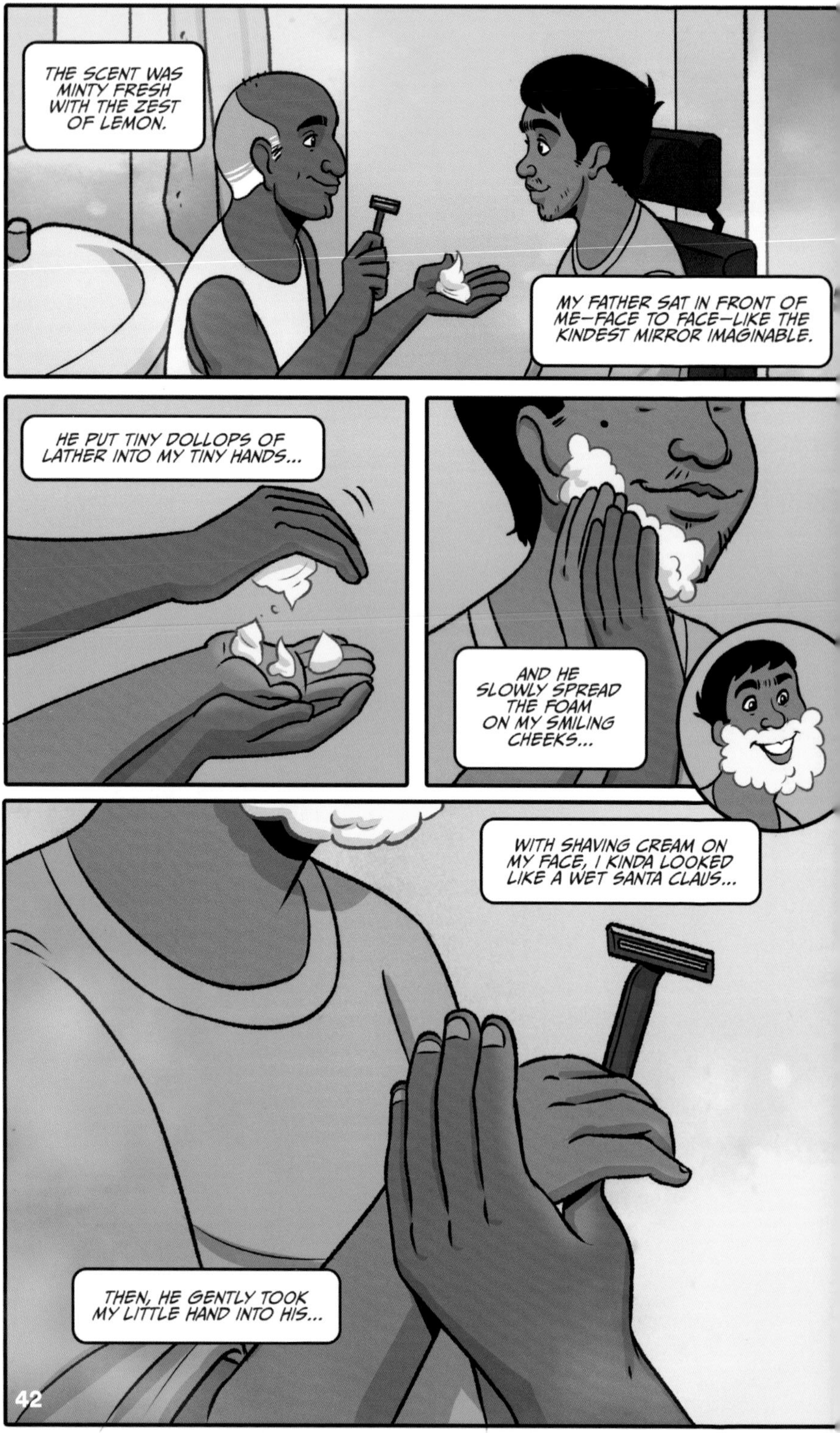
THE SCENT WAS MINTY FRESH WITH THE ZEST OF LEMON.
MY FATHER SAT IN FRONT OF ME—FACE TO FACE—LIKE THE KINDEST MIRROR IMAGINABLE.
HE PUT TINY DOLLOPS OF LATHER INTO MY TINY HANDS...
AND HE SLOWLY SPREAD THE FOAM ON MY SMILING CHEEKS...
WITH SHAVING CREAM ON MY FACE, I KINDA LOOKED LIKE A WET SANTA CLAUS...
THEN, HE GENTLY TOOK MY LITTLE HAND INTO HIS...

AND WITH GRACEFUL STROKES OF A DISPOSABLE RAZOR

WE SLOWLY SHAVED MY CHEEKS...

STROKE... RINSE... WIPE...

STROKE...

RINSE...

WIPE...

STROKE...

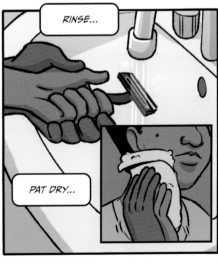

RINSE...

PAT DRY...

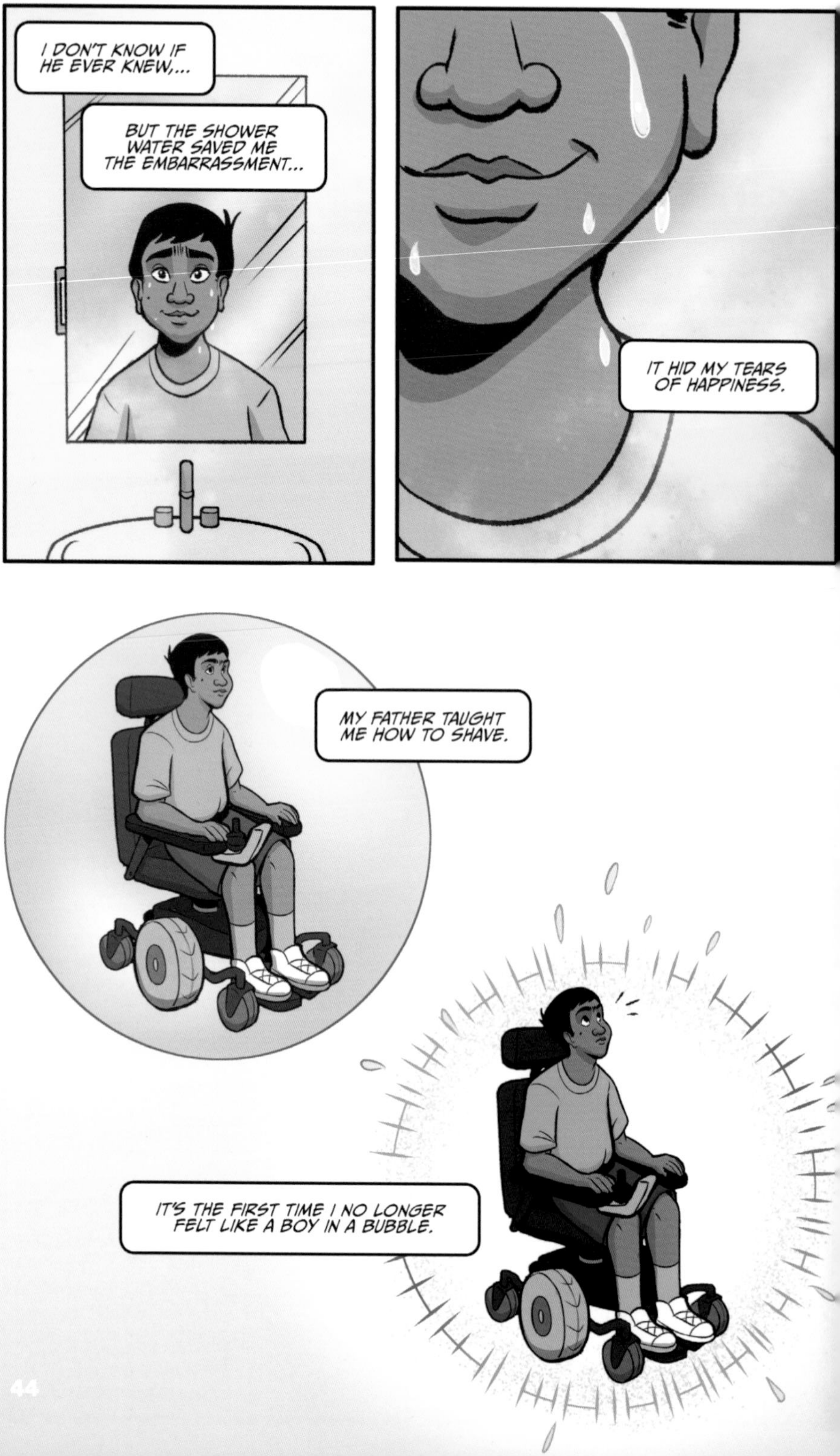
I DON'T KNOW IF HE EVER KNEW,...
BUT THE SHOWER WATER SAVED ME THE EMBARRASSMENT...
IT HID MY TEARS OF HAPPINESS.
MY FATHER TAUGHT ME HOW TO SHAVE.
IT'S THE FIRST TIME I NO LONGER FELT LIKE A BOY IN A BUBBLE.

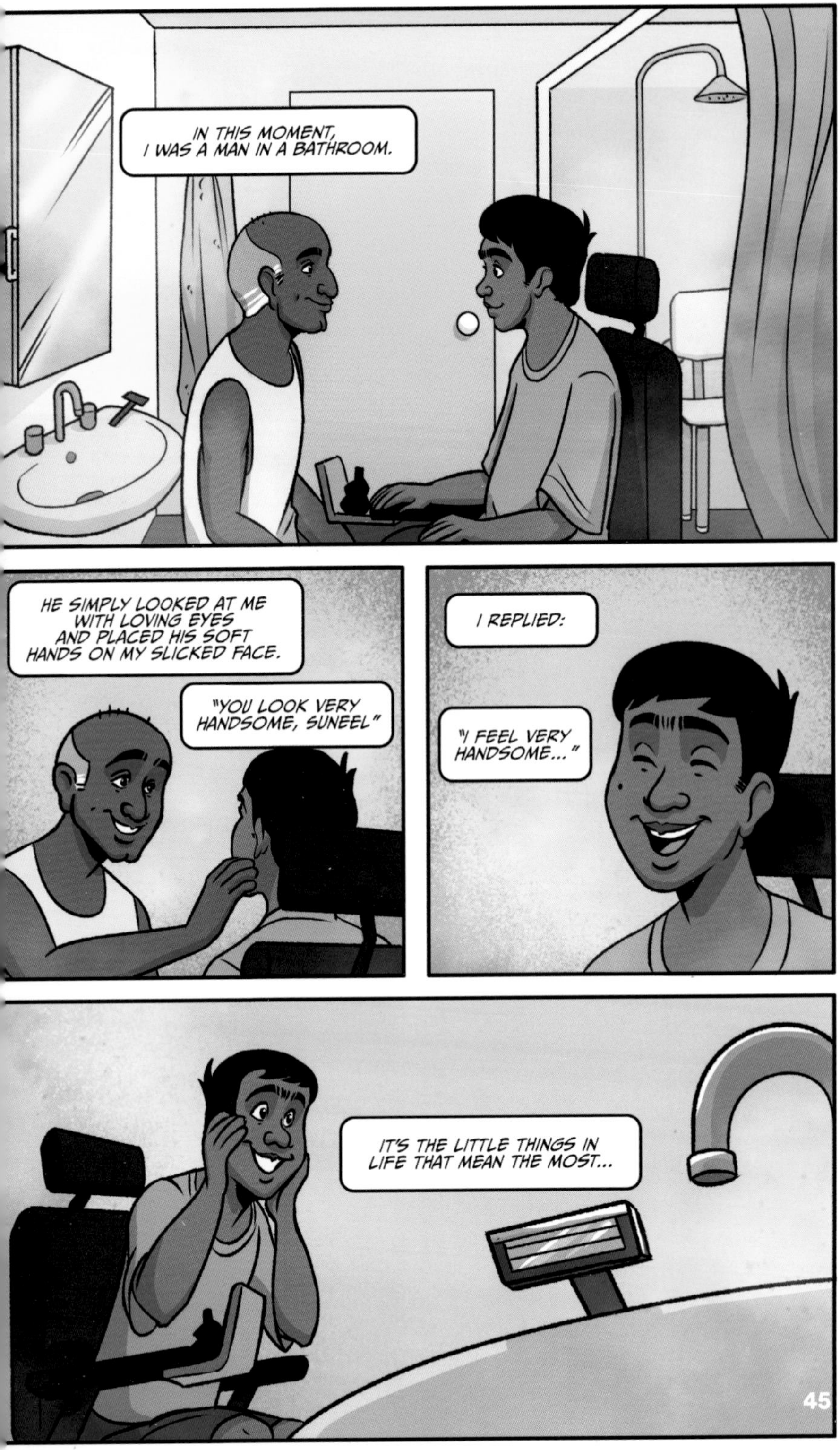
IN THIS MOMENT, I WAS A MAN IN A BATHROOM.
HE SIMPLY LOOKED AT ME WITH LOVING EYES AND PLACED HIS SOFT HANDS ON MY SLICKED FACE.
"YOU LOOK VERY HANDSOME, SUNEEL"
I REPLIED:
"I FEEL VERY HANDSOME..."
IT'S THE LITTLE THINGS IN LIFE THAT MEAN THE MOST...

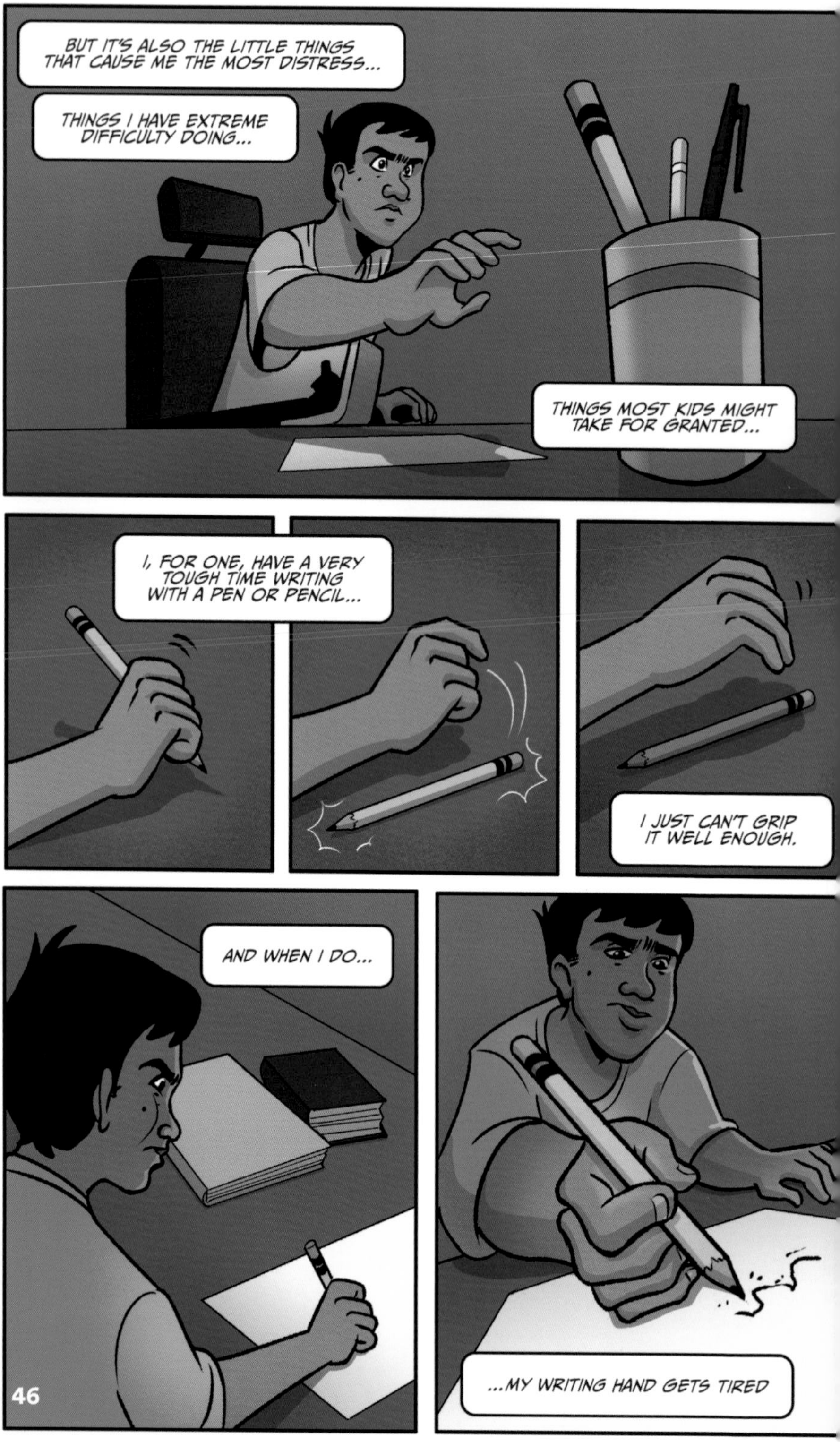
BUT IT'S ALSO THE LITTLE THINGS THAT CAUSE ME THE MOST DISTRESS...
THINGS I HAVE EXTREME DIFFICULTY DOING...
THINGS MOST KIDS MIGHT TAKE FOR GRANTED...
I, FOR ONE, HAVE A VERY TOUGH TIME WRITING WITH A PEN OR PENCIL...
I JUST CAN'T GRIP IT WELL ENOUGH.
AND WHEN I DO...
...MY WRITING HAND GETS TIRED

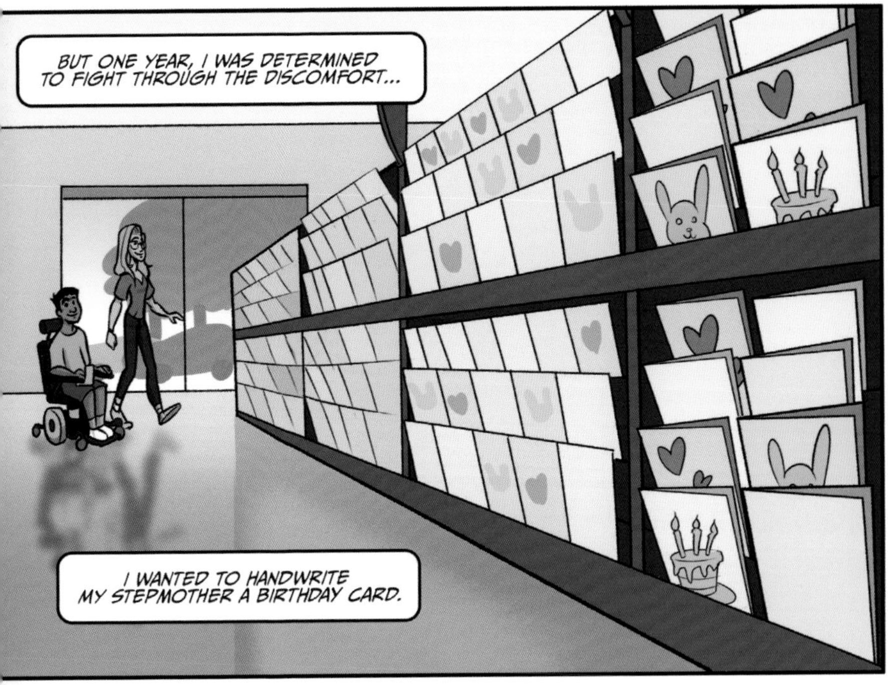
BUT ONE YEAR, I WAS DETERMINED TO FIGHT THROUGH THE DISCOMFORT...
I WANTED TO HANDWRITE MY STEPMOTHER A BIRTHDAY CARD.

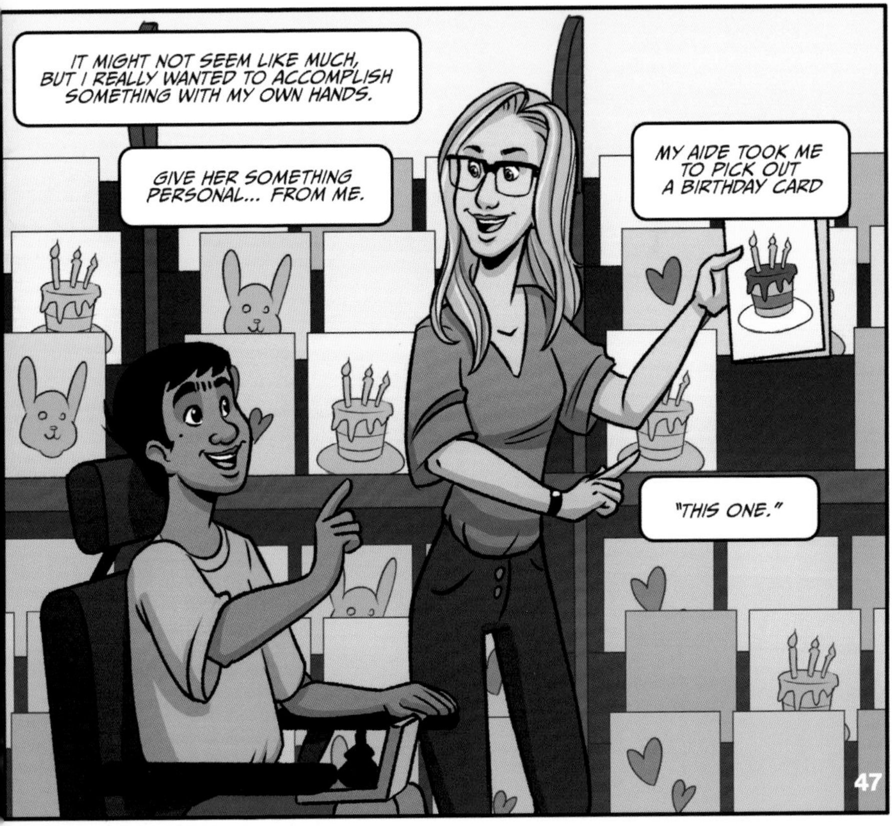
IT MIGHT NOT SEEM LIKE MUCH, BUT I REALLY WANTED TO ACCOMPLISH SOMETHING WITH MY OWN HANDS.
GIVE HER SOMETHING PERSONAL... FROM ME.
MY AIDE TOOK ME TO PICK OUT A BIRTHDAY CARD
"THIS ONE."

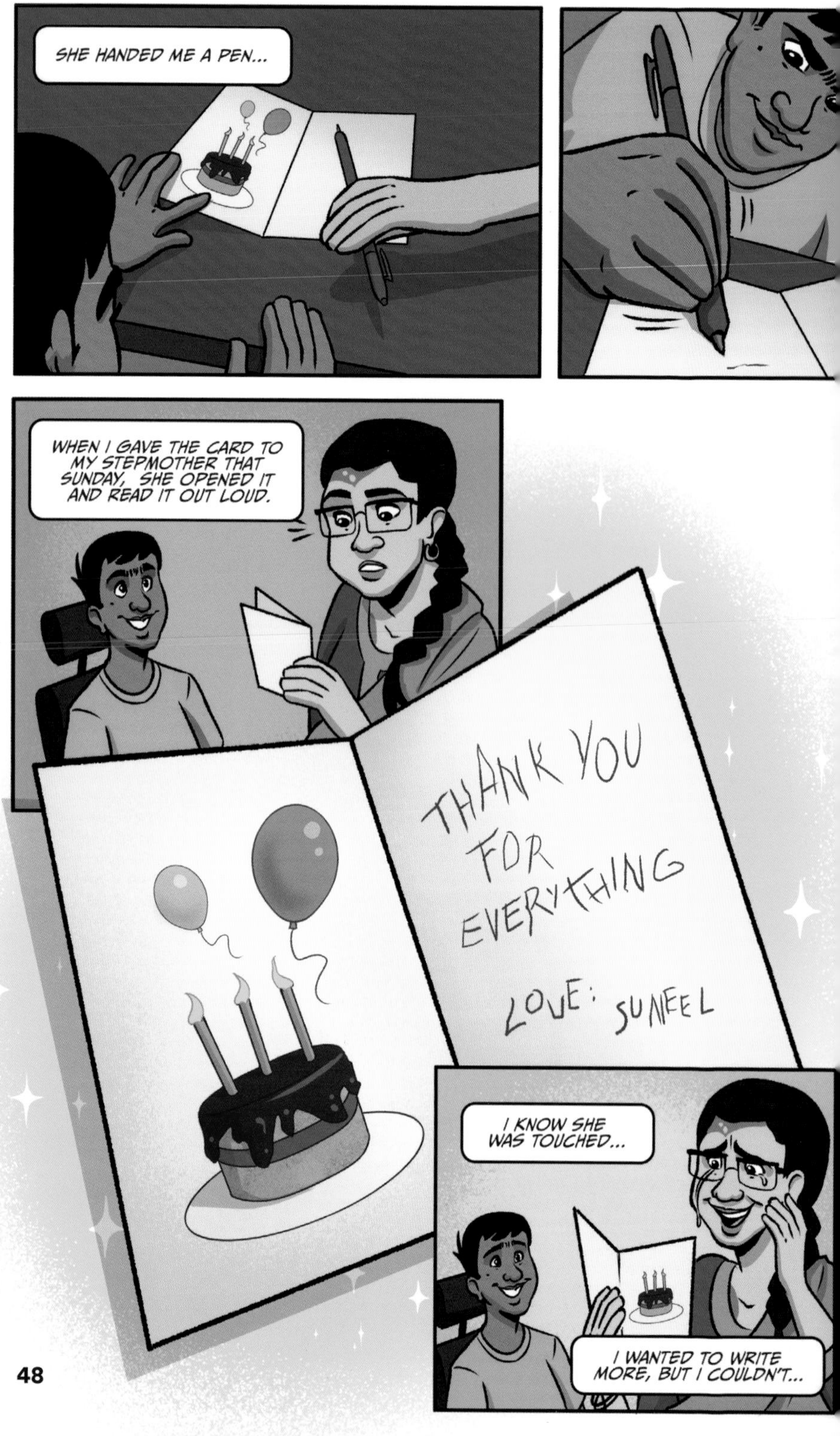
SHE HANDED ME A PEN...
WHEN I GAVE THE CARD TO MY STEPMOTHER THAT SUNDAY, SHE OPENED IT AND READ IT OUT LOUD.
THANK YOU FOR EVERYTHING
LOVE: SUNEEL
I KNOW SHE WAS TOUCHED...
I WANTED TO WRITE MORE, BUT I COULDN'T...

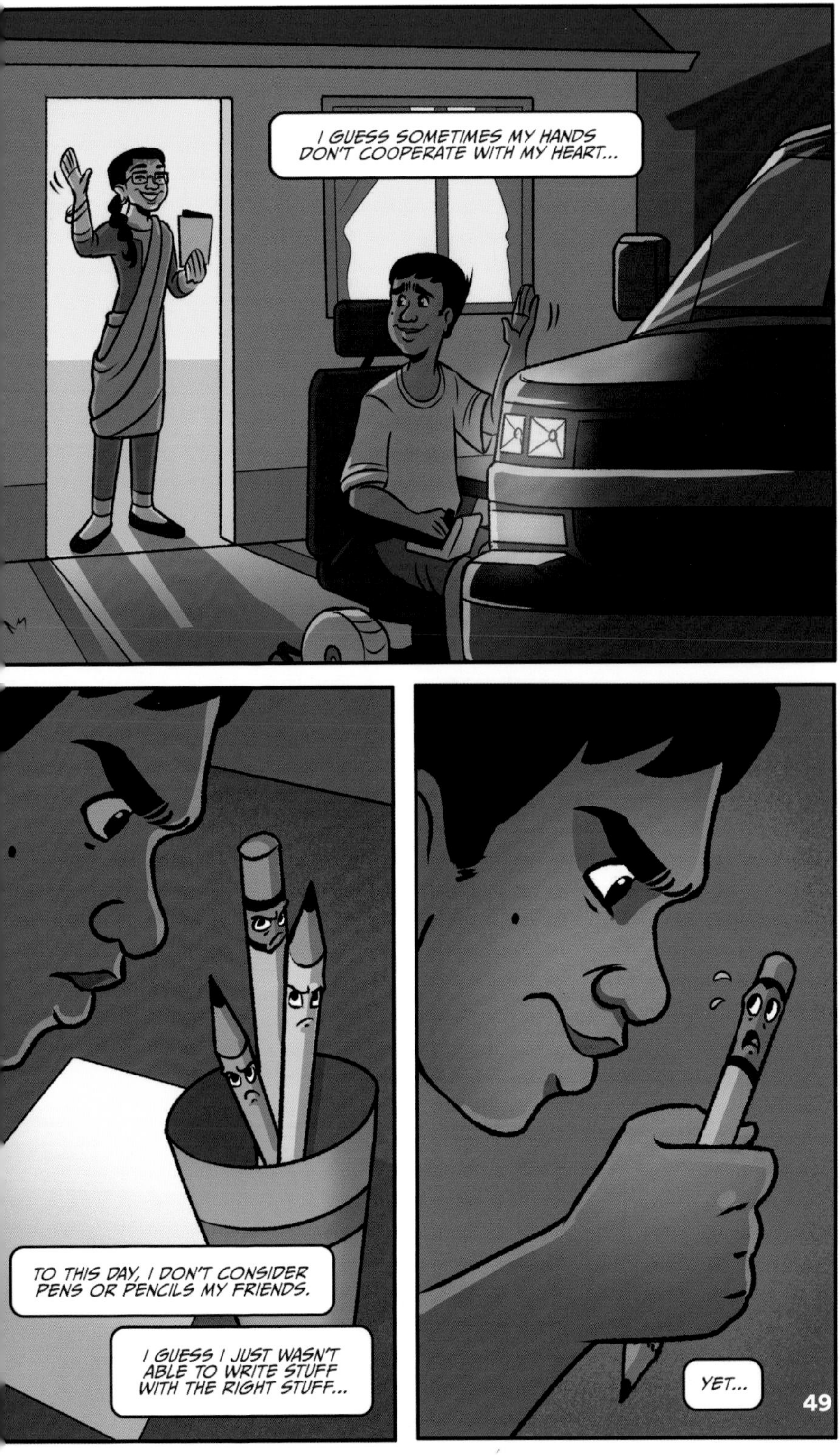
I GUESS SOMETIMES MY HANDS DON'T COOPERATE WITH MY HEART...
TO THIS DAY, I DON'T CONSIDER PENS OR PENCILS MY FRIENDS.
I GUESS I JUST WASN'T ABLE TO WRITE STUFF WITH THE RIGHT STUFF...
YET...

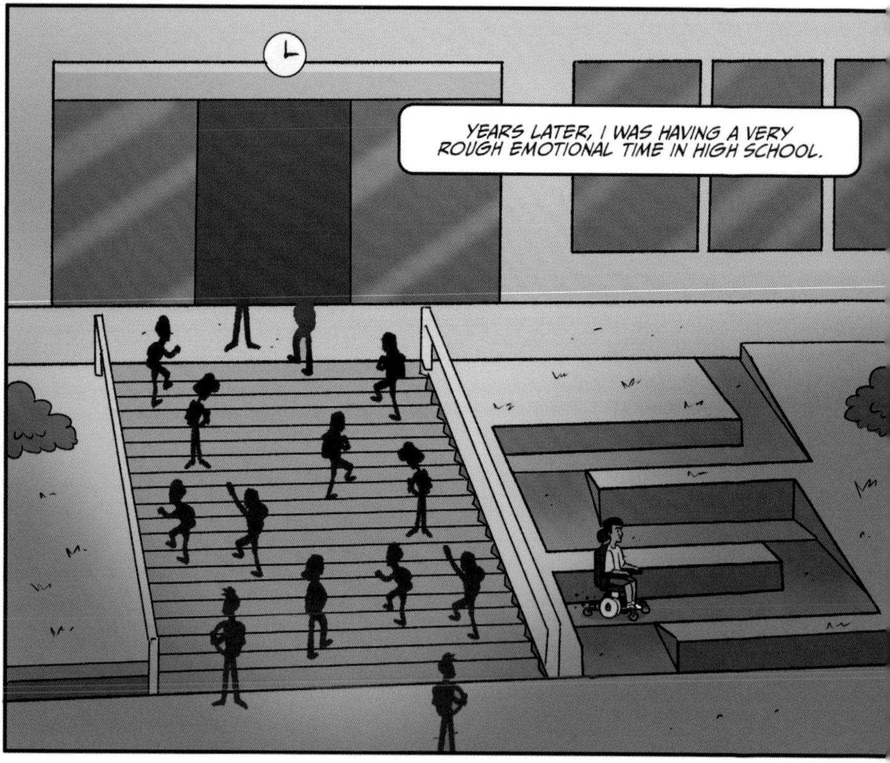
YEARS LATER, I WAS HAVING A VERY ROUGH EMOTIONAL TIME IN HIGH SCHOOL.

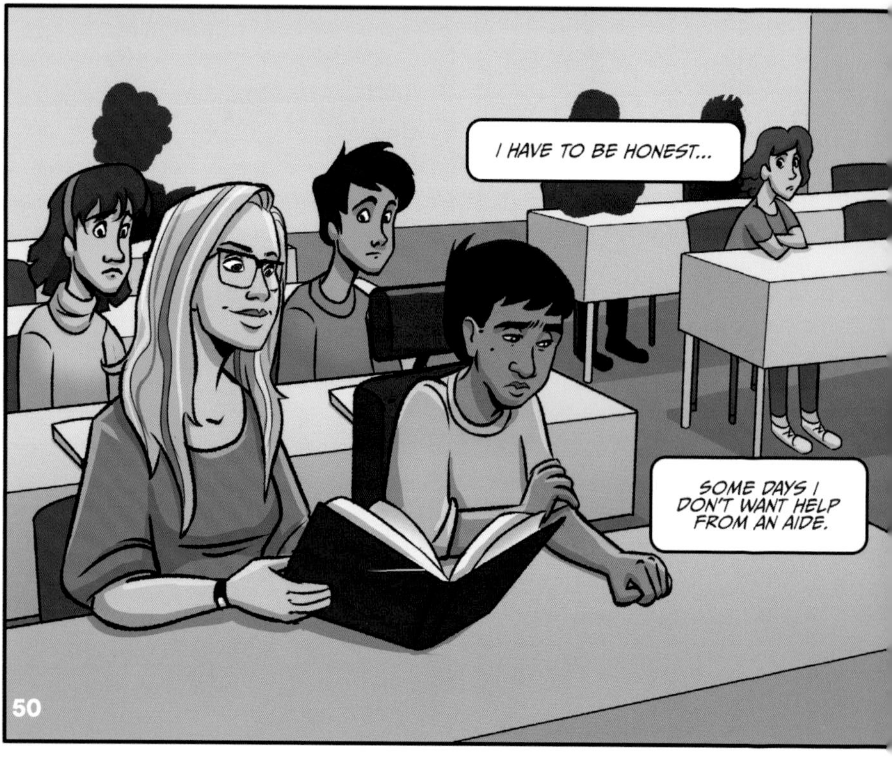
I HAVE TO BE HONEST...
SOME DAYS I DON'T WANT HELP FROM AN AIDE.

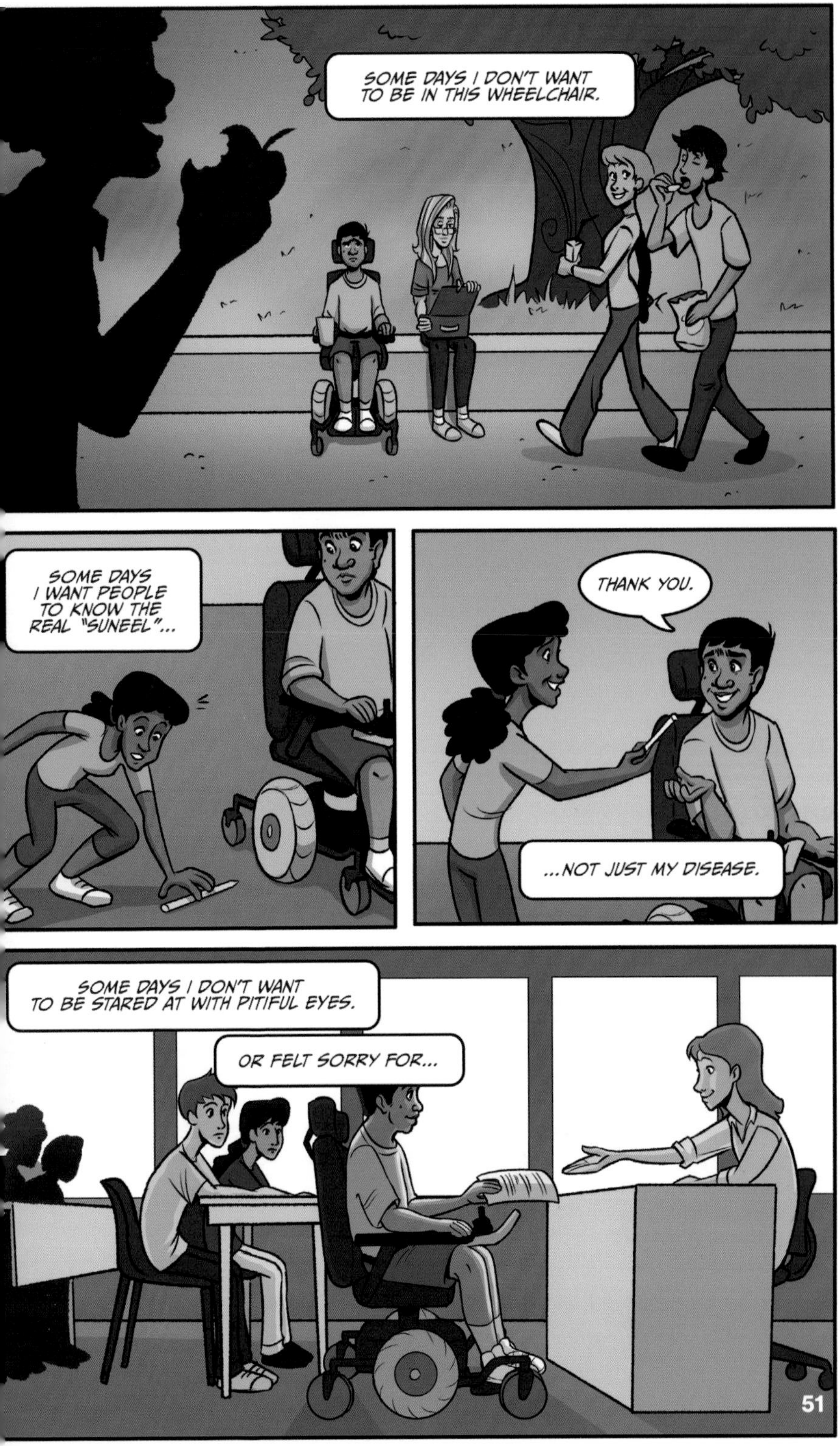
SOME DAYS I DON'T WANT TO BE IN THIS WHEELCHAIR.
SOME DAYS I WANT PEOPLE TO KNOW THE REAL "SUNEEL"...
THANK YOU.
...NOT JUST MY DISEASE.
SOME DAYS I DON'T WANT TO BE STARED AT WITH PITIFUL EYES.
OR FELT SORRY FOR...

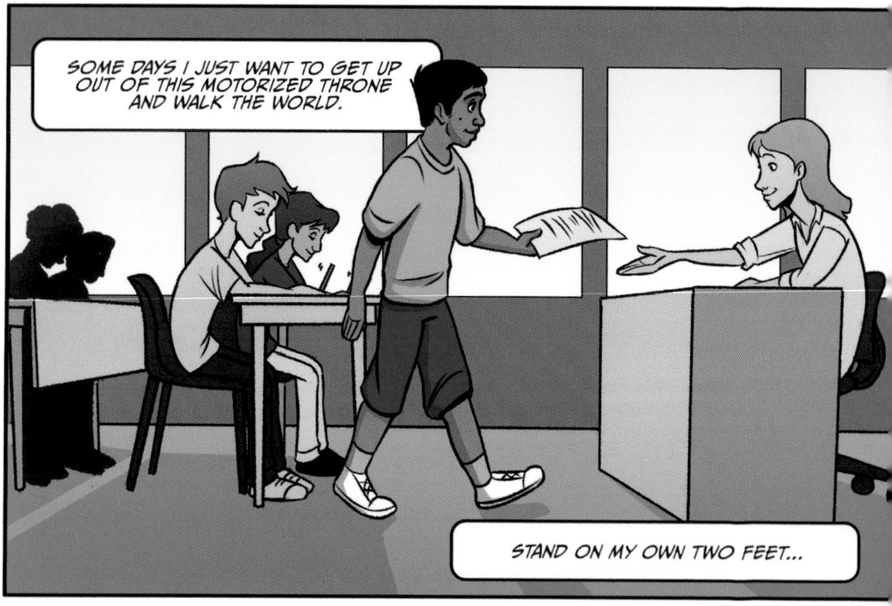
SOME DAYS I JUST WANT TO GET UP OUT OF THIS MOTORIZED THRONE AND WALK THE WORLD.
STAND ON MY OWN TWO FEET...

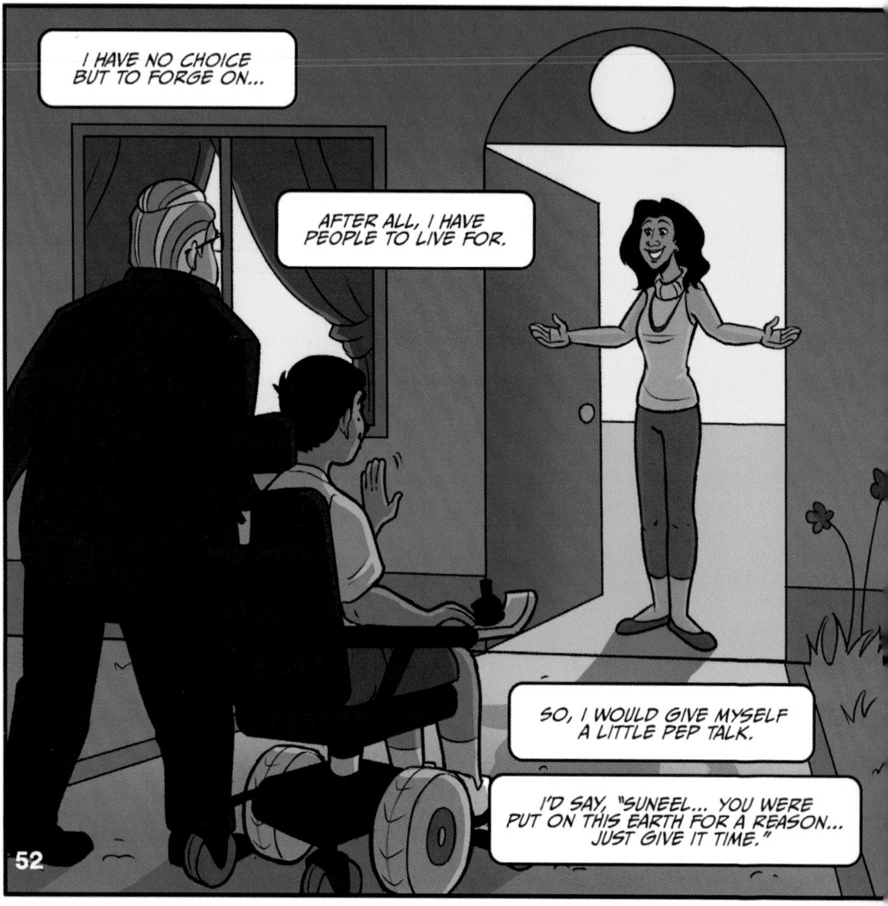
I HAVE NO CHOICE BUT TO FORGE ON...
AFTER ALL, I HAVE PEOPLE TO LIVE FOR.
SO, I WOULD GIVE MYSELF A LITTLE PEP TALK.
I'D SAY, "SUNEEL... YOU WERE PUT ON THIS EARTH FOR A REASON... JUST GIVE IT TIME."

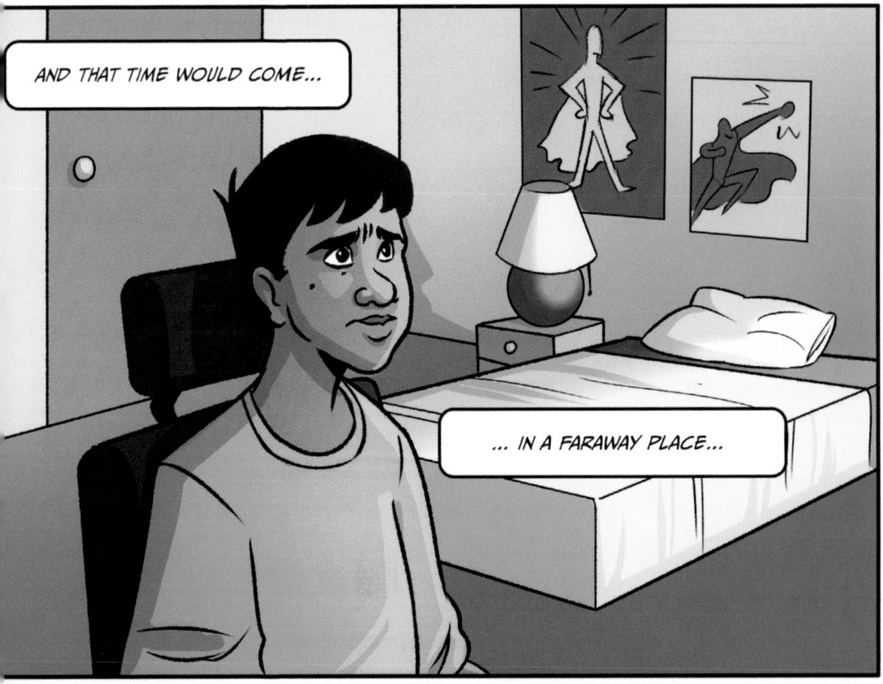
AND THAT TIME WOULD COME...
... IN A FARAWAY PLACE...

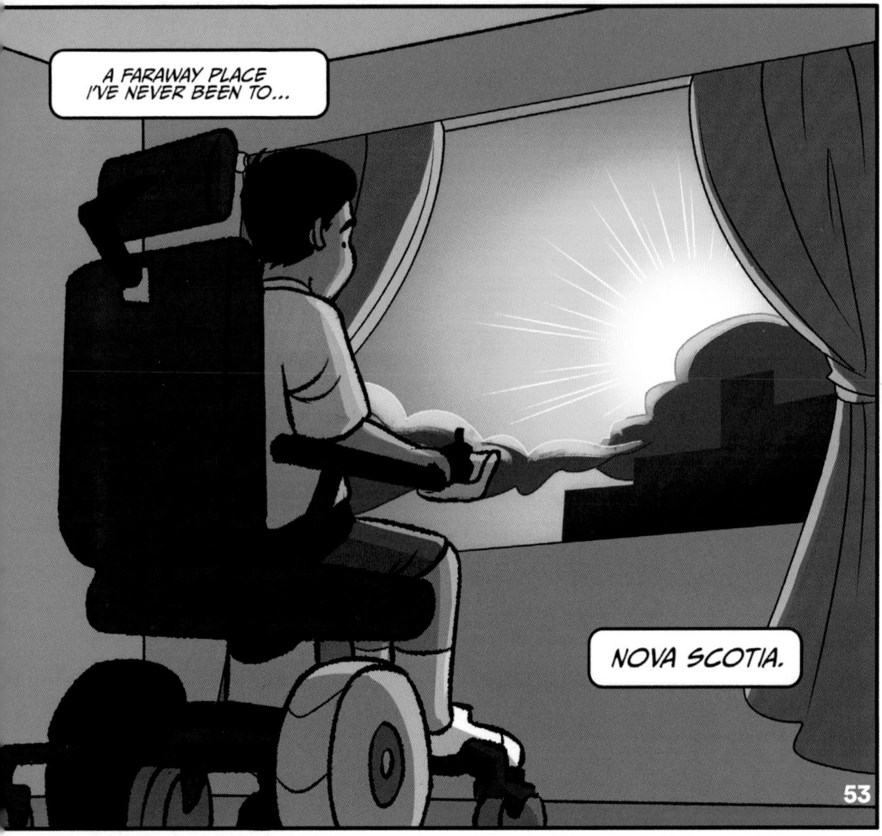
A FARAWAY PLACE I'VE NEVER BEEN TO...
NOVA SCOTIA.

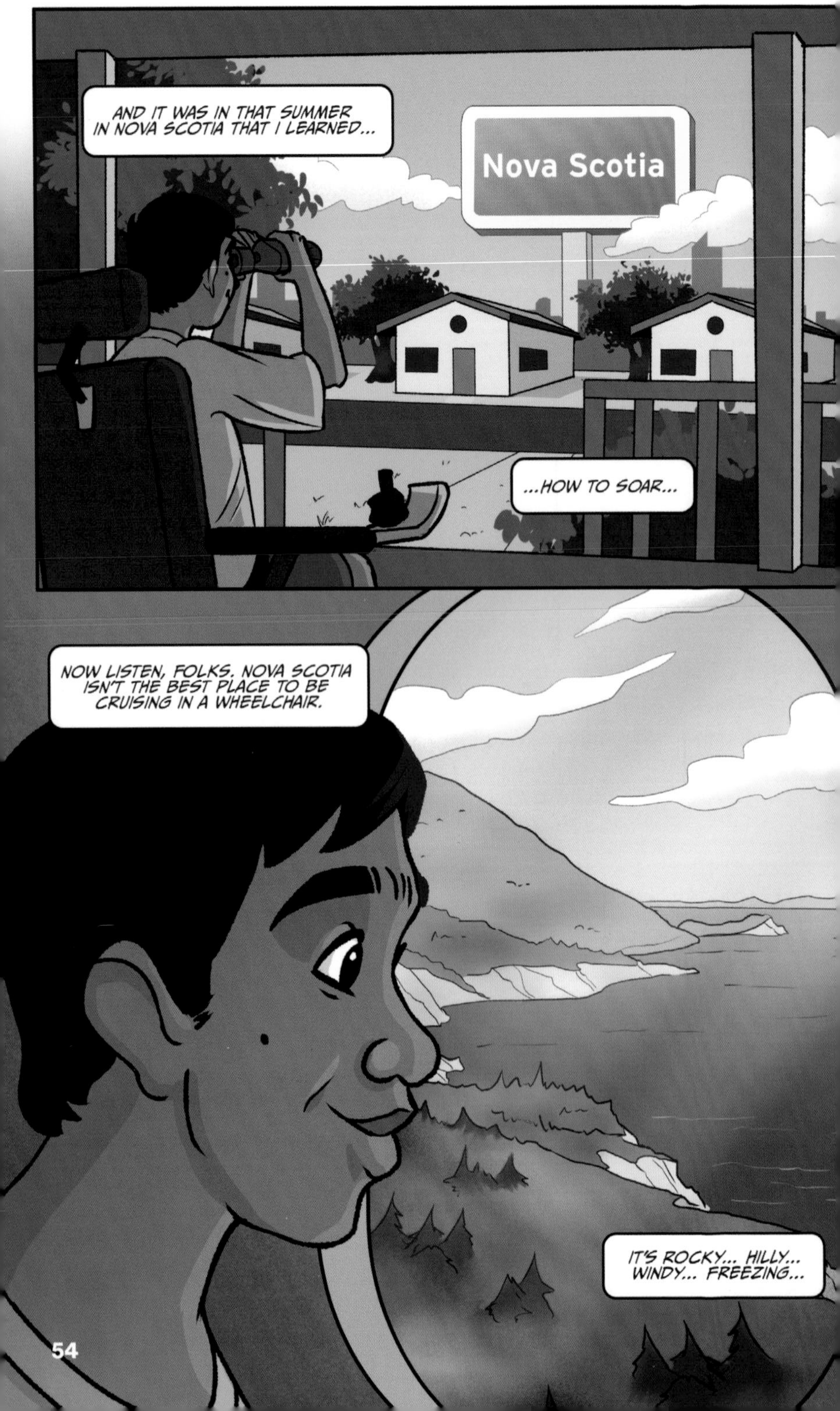
AND IT WAS IN THAT SUMMER IN NOVA SCOTIA THAT I LEARNED...
Nova Scotia
...HOW TO SOAR...
NOW LISTEN, FOLKS. NOVA SCOTIA ISN'T THE BEST PLACE TO BE CRUISING IN A WHEELCHAIR.
IT'S ROCKY... HILLY... WINDY... FREEZING...

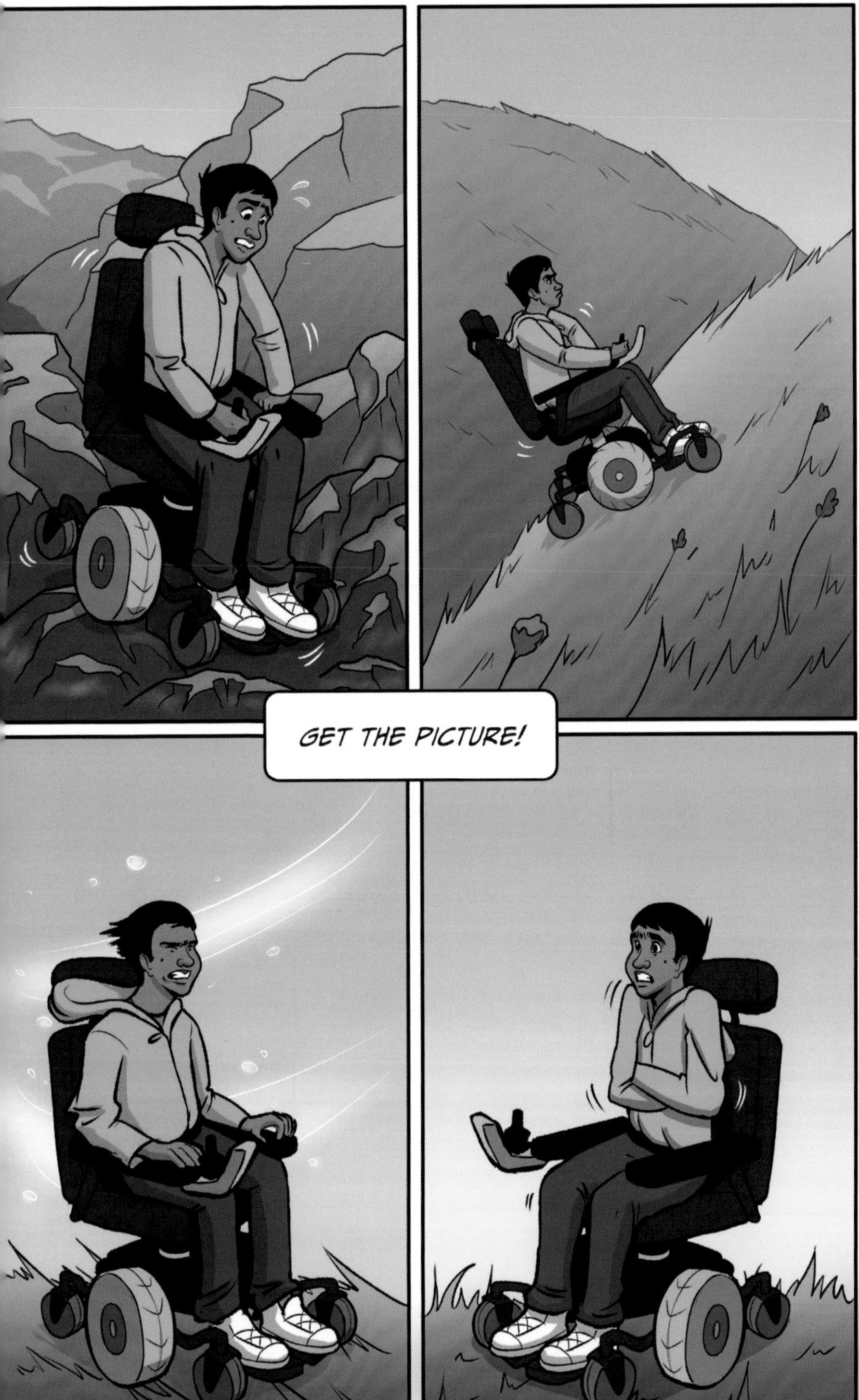
GET THE PICTURE!

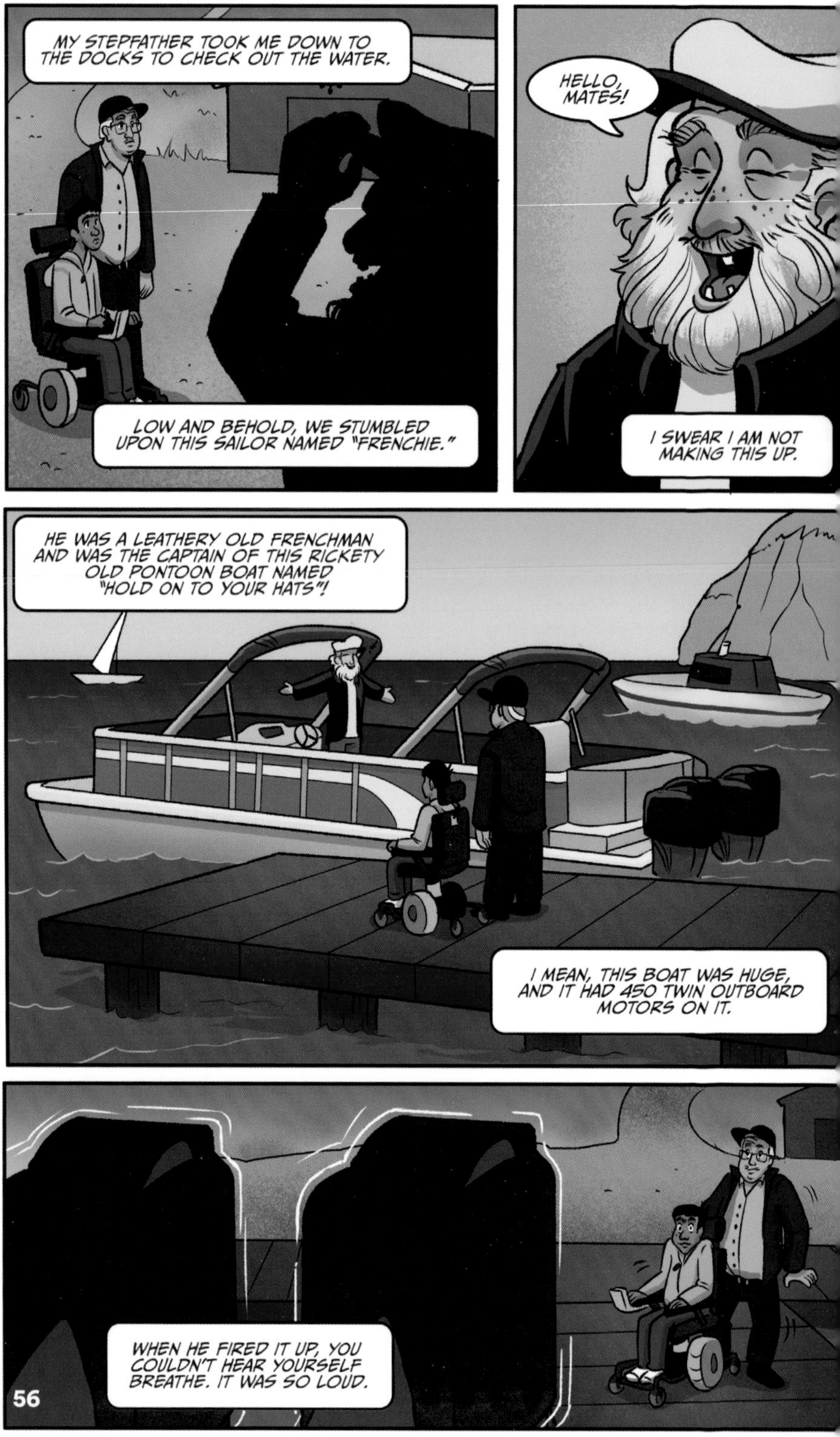

MY STEPFATHER TOOK ME DOWN TO THE DOCKS TO CHECK OUT THE WATER.
LOW AND BEHOLD, WE STUMBLED UPON THIS SAILOR NAMED "FRENCHIE."
HELLO, MATES!
I SWEAR I AM NOT MAKING THIS UP.
HE WAS A LEATHERY OLD FRENCHMAN AND WAS THE CAPTAIN OF THIS RICKETY OLD PONTOON BOAT NAMED "HOLD ON TO YOUR HATS"!
I MEAN, THIS BOAT WAS HUGE, AND IT HAD 450 TWIN OUTBOARD MOTORS ON IT.
WHEN HE FIRED IT UP, YOU COULDN'T HEAR YOURSELF BREATHE. IT WAS SO LOUD.

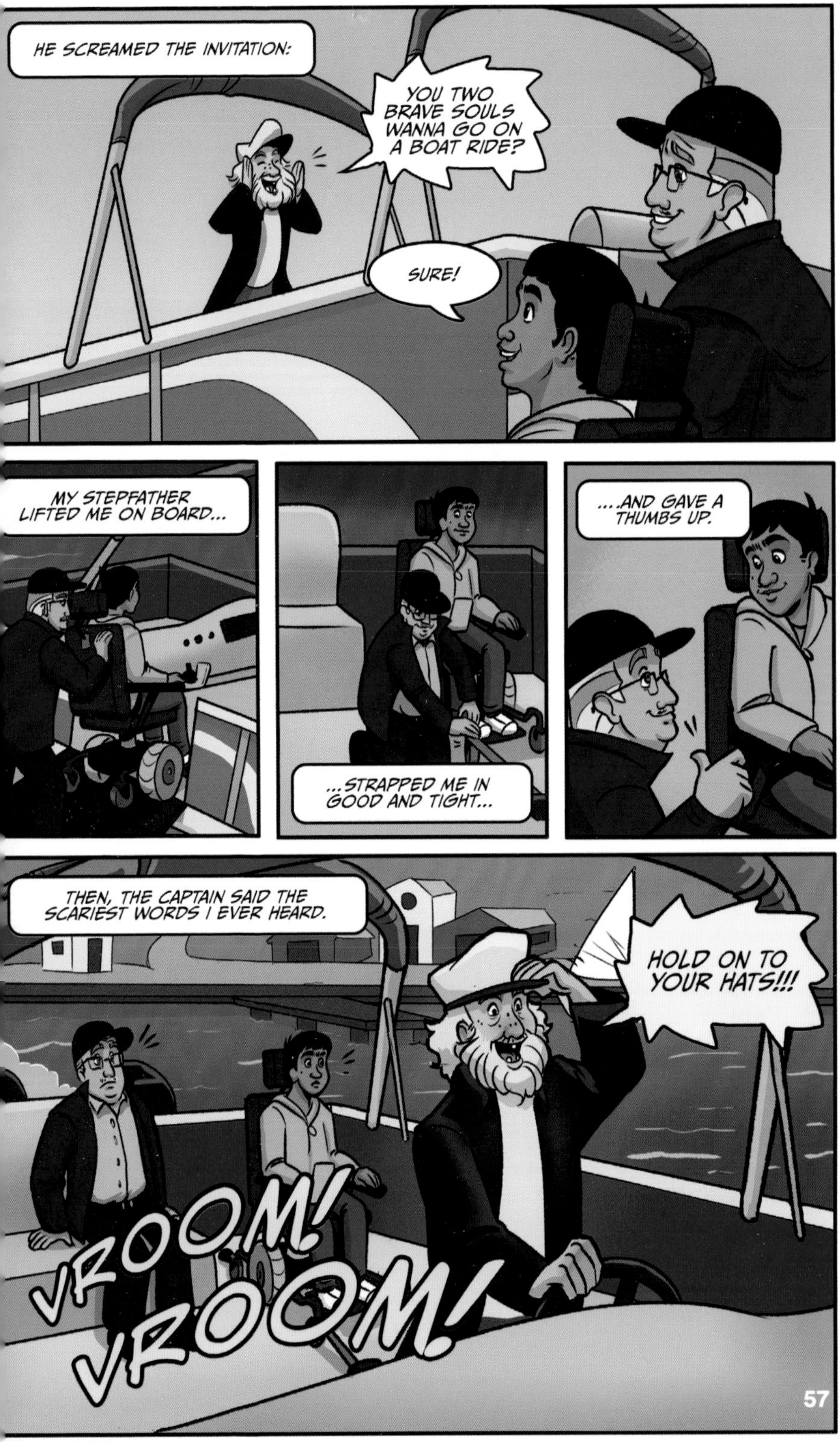
HE SCREAMED THE INVITATION:
YOU TWO BRAVE SOULS WANNA GO ON A BOAT RIDE?
SURE!
MY STEPFATHER LIFTED ME ON BOARD...
...STRAPPED ME IN GOOD AND TIGHT...
....AND GAVE A THUMBS UP.
THEN, THE CAPTAIN SAID THE SCARIEST WORDS I EVER HEARD.
HOLD ON TO YOUR HATS!!!
VROOM! VROOM!

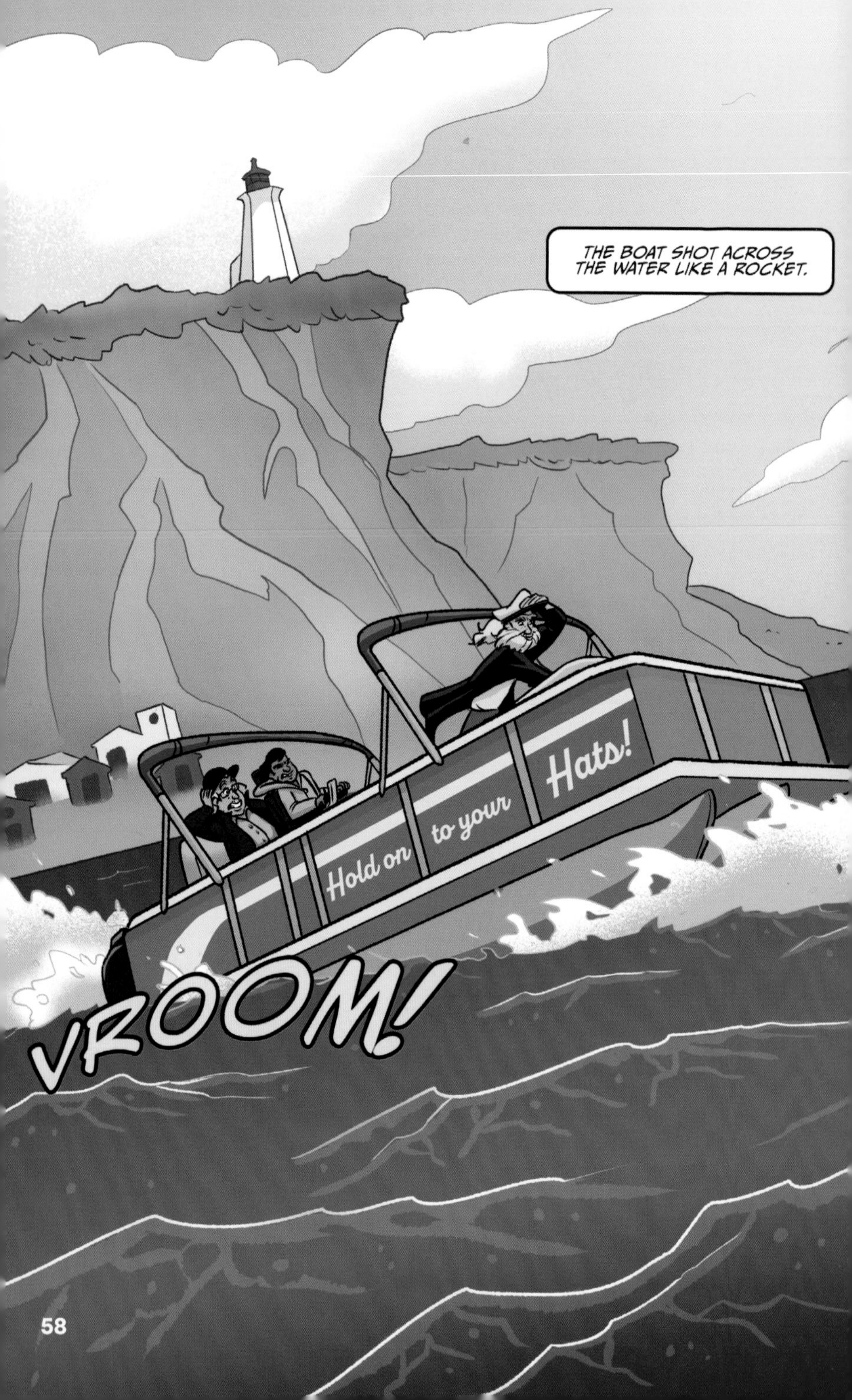
THE BOAT SHOT ACROSS THE WATER LIKE A ROCKET.
Hold on to your Hats!
VROOM!

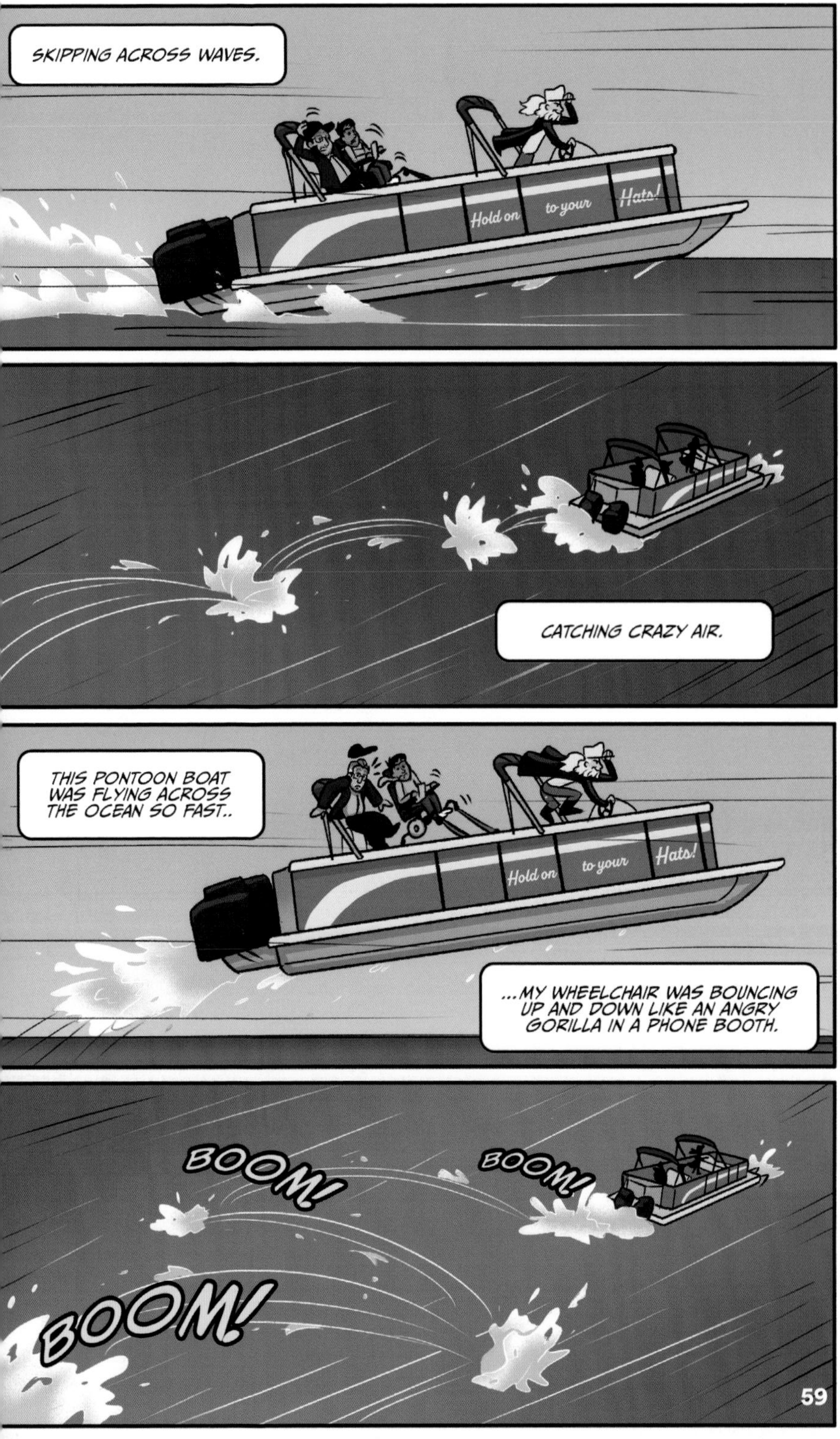
SKIPPING ACROSS WAVES.
Hold on to your Hats!
CATCHING CRAZY AIR.
THIS PONTOON BOAT WAS FLYING ACROSS THE OCEAN SO FAST..
Hold on to your Hats!
...MY WHEELCHAIR WAS BOUNCING UP AND DOWN LIKE AN ANGRY GORILLA IN A PHONE BOOTH.
BOOM!
BOOM!
BOOM!

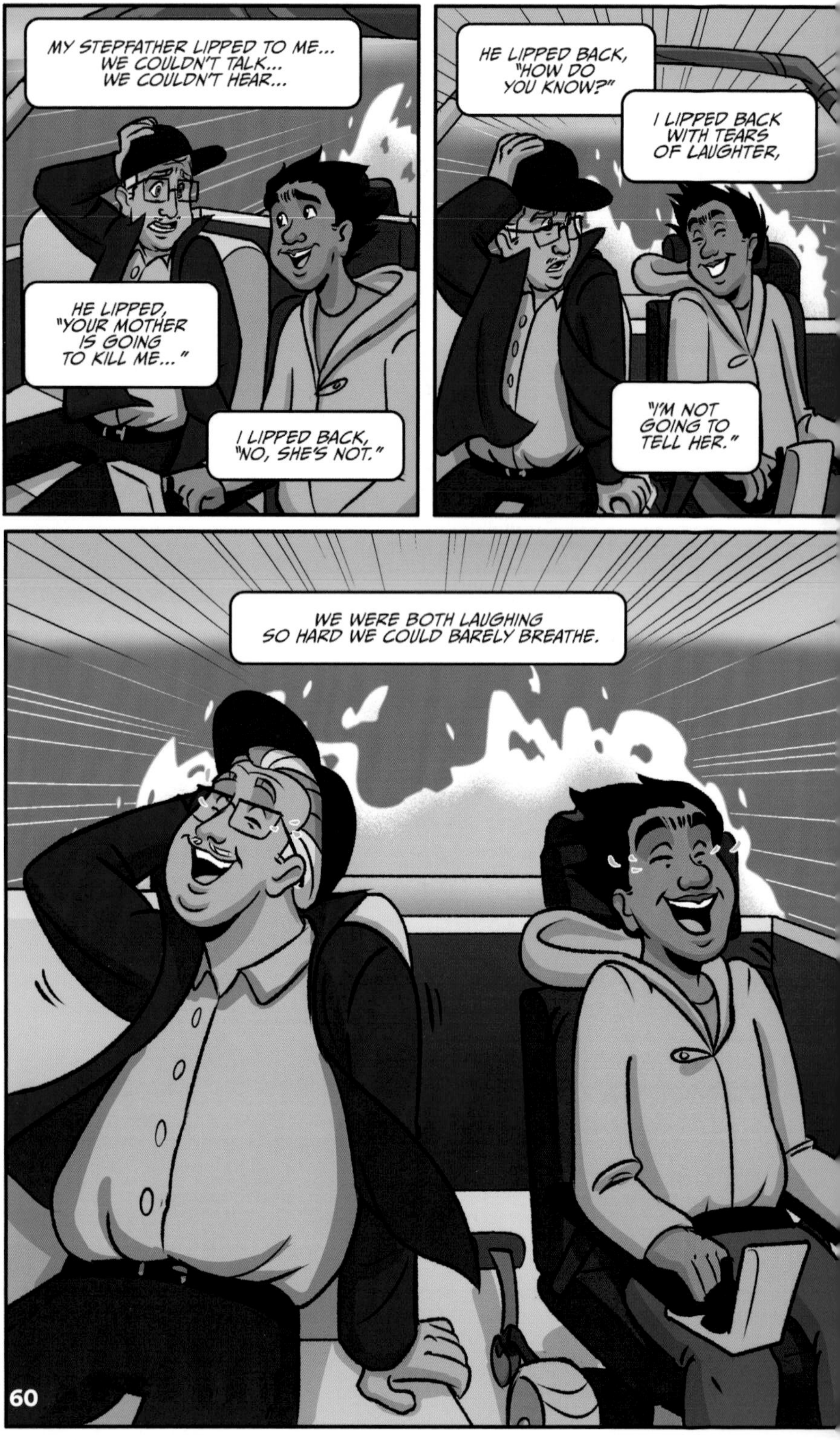
MY STEPFATHER LIPPED TO ME... WE COULDN'T TALK... WE COULDN'T HEAR...
HE LIPPED, "YOUR MOTHER IS GOING TO KILL ME..."
I LIPPED BACK, "NO, SHE'S NOT."
HE LIPPED BACK, "HOW DO YOU KNOW?"
I LIPPED BACK WITH TEARS OF LAUGHTER,
"I'M NOT GOING TO TELL HER."
WE WERE BOTH LAUGHING SO HARD WE COULD BARELY BREATHE.

AS I LOOKED OVER THE SIDE, I COULD ACTUALLY SEE SHARK FINS AND SWIMMING SEALS.

IT WAS LIKE A WHOLE NEW WORLD DOWN THERE.

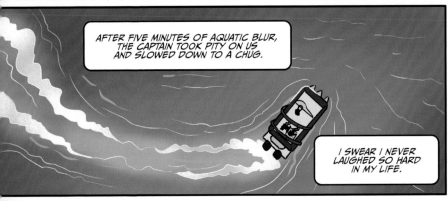

AFTER FIVE MINUTES OF AQUATIC BLUR, THE CAPTAIN TOOK PITY ON US AND SLOWED DOWN TO A CHUG.

I SWEAR I NEVER LAUGHED SO HARD IN MY LIFE.

ONE THING ABOUT LAUGHTER TEARS... THEY MAKE UP FOR THE SAD ONES...

ON OUR WAY BACK, I LOOKED UP...

...AND SAW THE MOST BEAUTIFUL THING IN MY LIFE.

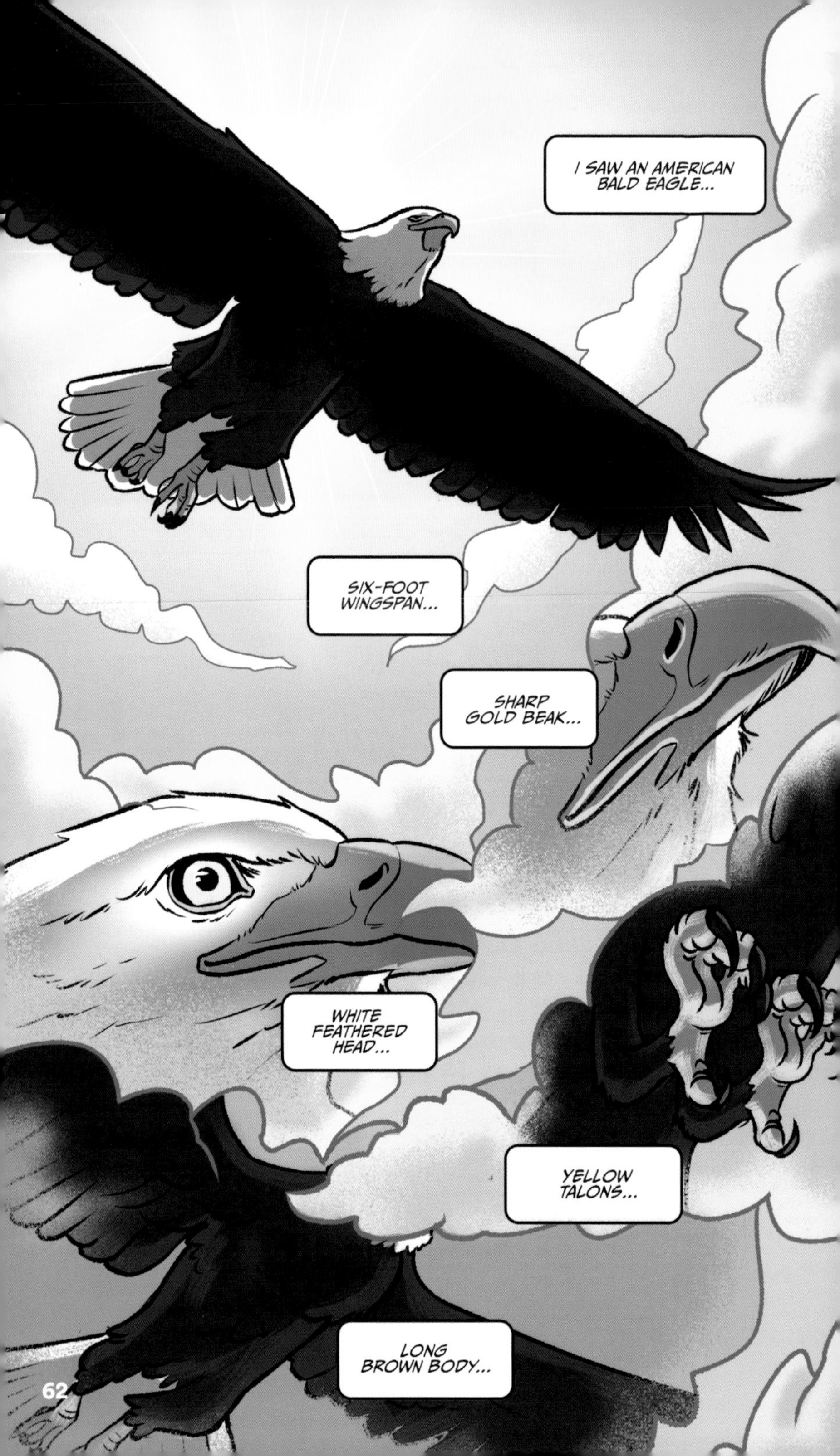
I SAW AN AMERICAN BALD EAGLE...
SIX-FOOT WINGSPAN...
SHARP GOLD BEAK...
WHITE FEATHERED HEAD...
YELLOW TALONS...
LONG BROWN BODY...

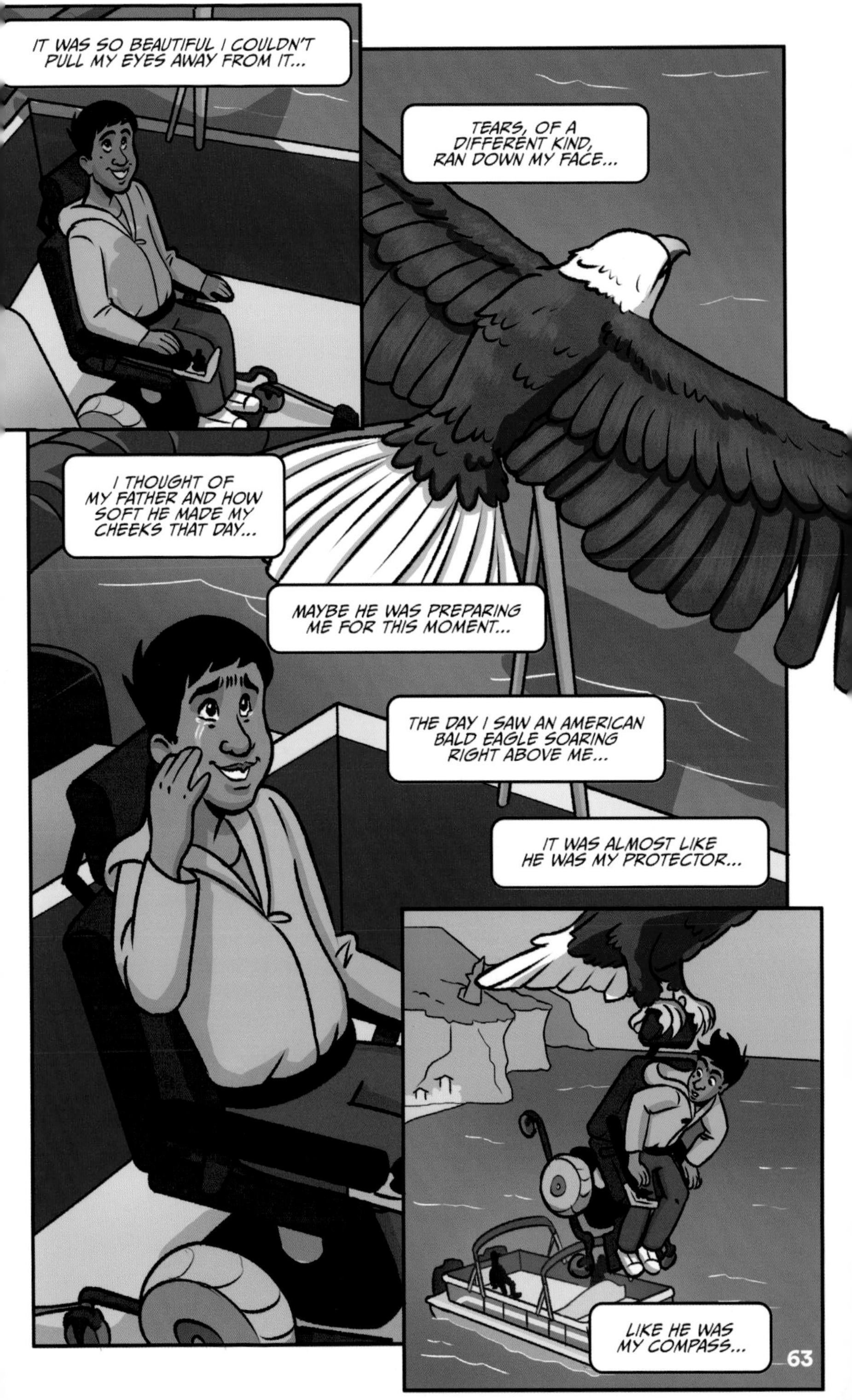
IT WAS SO BEAUTIFUL I COULDN'T PULL MY EYES AWAY FROM IT...
TEARS, OF A DIFFERENT KIND, RAN DOWN MY FACE...
I THOUGHT OF MY FATHER AND HOW SOFT HE MADE MY CHEEKS THAT DAY...
MAYBE HE WAS PREPARING ME FOR THIS MOMENT...
THE DAY I SAW AN AMERICAN BALD EAGLE SOARING RIGHT ABOVE ME...
IT WAS ALMOST LIKE HE WAS MY PROTECTOR...
LIKE HE WAS MY COMPASS...

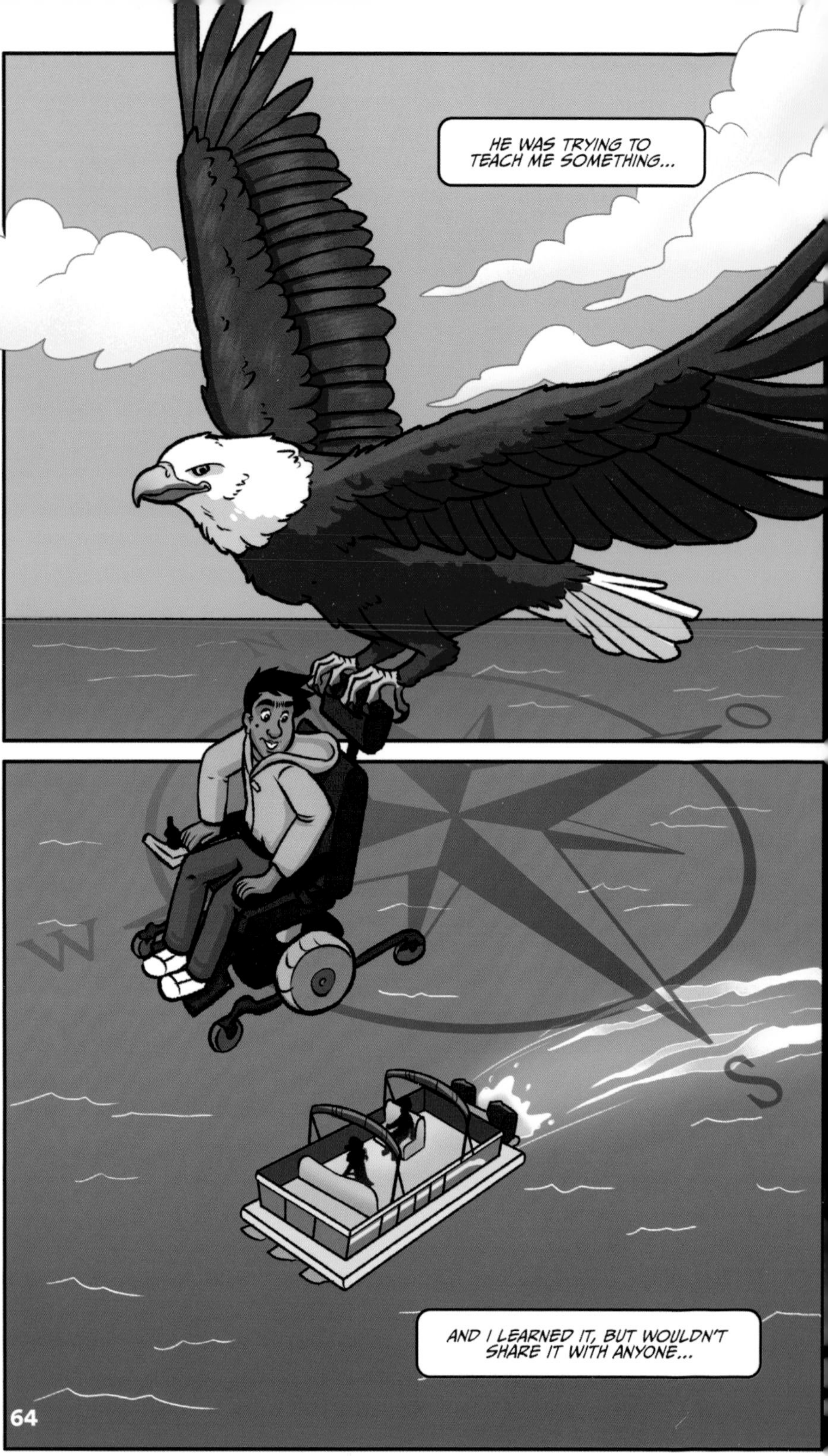
HE WAS TRYING TO TEACH ME SOMETHING...
W
S
AND I LEARNED IT, BUT WOULDN'T SHARE IT WITH ANYONE...

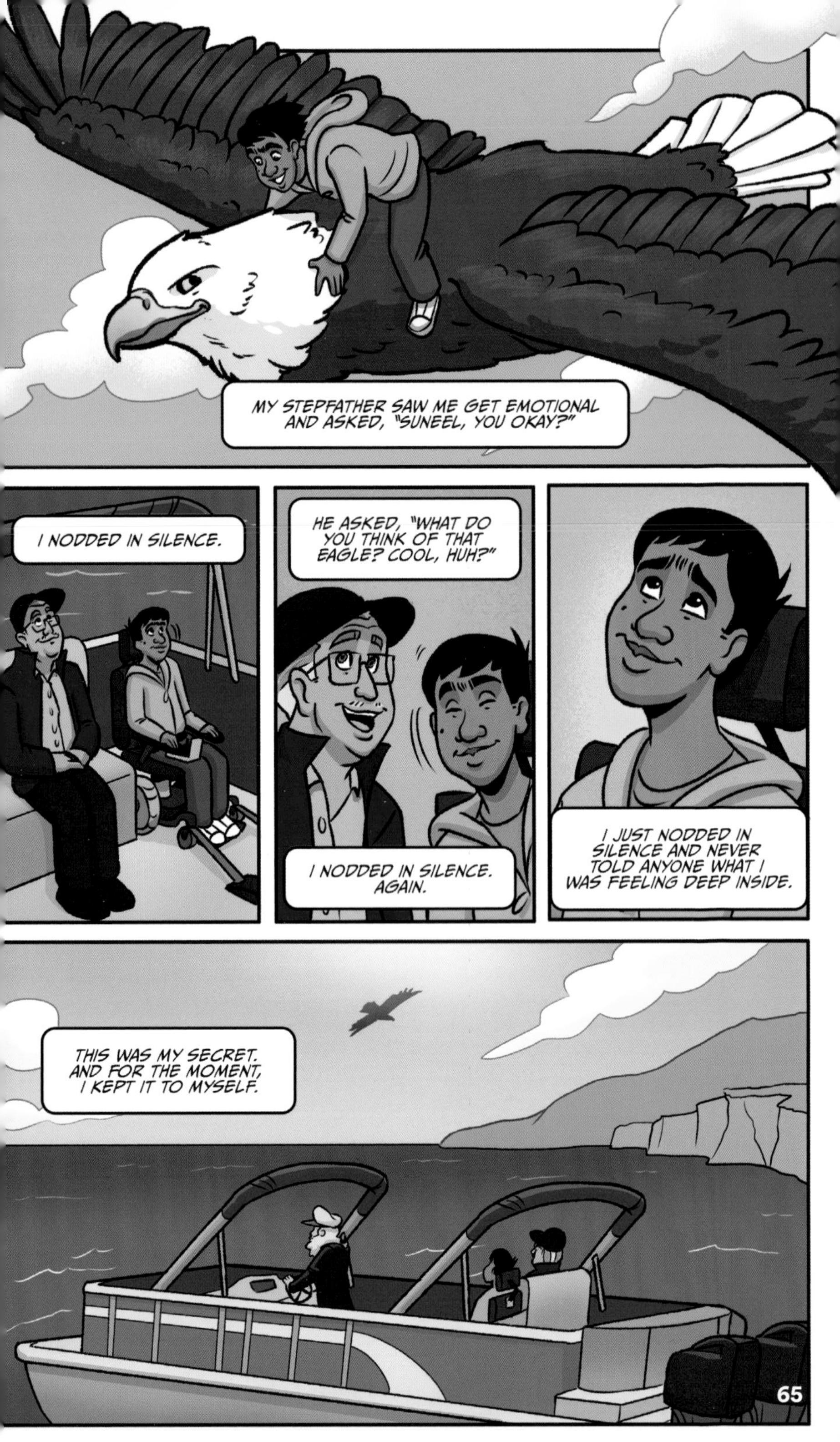
MY STEPFATHER SAW ME GET EMOTIONAL AND ASKED, "SUNEEL, YOU OKAY?"
I NODDED IN SILENCE.
HE ASKED, "WHAT DO YOU THINK OF THAT EAGLE? COOL, HUH?"
I NODDED IN SILENCE. AGAIN.
I JUST NODDED IN SILENCE AND NEVER TOLD ANYONE WHAT I WAS FEELING DEEP INSIDE.
THIS WAS MY SECRET. AND FOR THE MOMENT, I KEPT IT TO MYSELF.

WHEN I GOT BACK TO BUFFALO, MY LIFE WAS NEVER THE SAME AFTER THAT DAY IN NOVA SCOTIA.

I DID WELL IN HIGH SCHOOL AND FORGED ON TO COLLEGE.

I WAS DETERMINED TO TAKE ON ALL THAT LIFE HAD IN STORE FOR ME.

GOOD OR BAD.

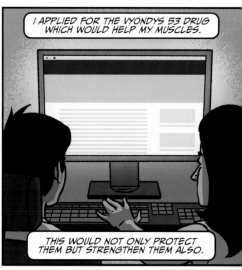

I APPLIED FOR THE VYONDYS 53 DRUG WHICH WOULD HELP MY MUSCLES.

THIS WOULD NOT ONLY PROTECT THEM BUT STRENGTHEN THEM ALSO.

I MEAN... THIS DRUG WOULD REALLY HELP ME.

I WAS DENIED.

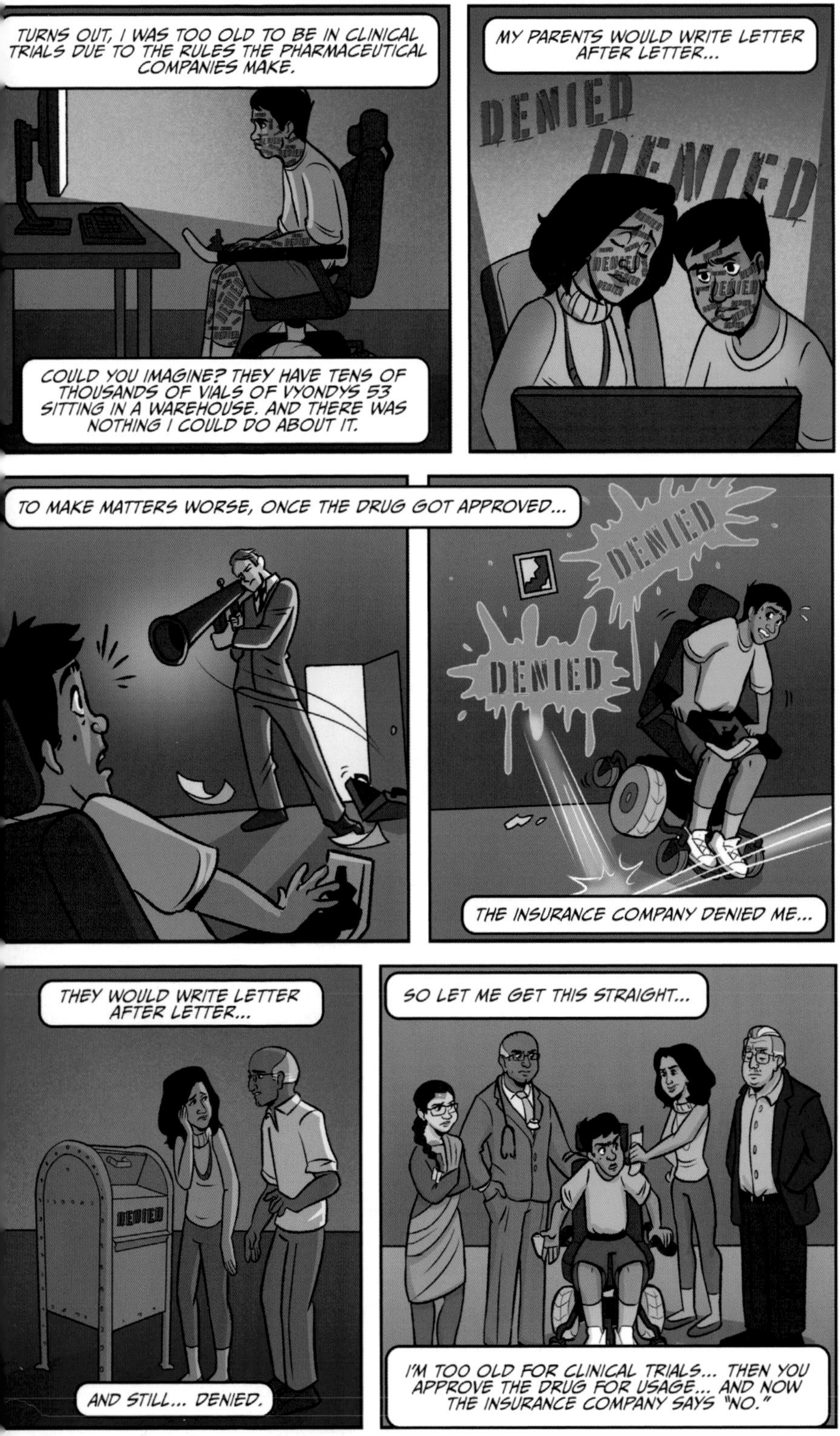
TURNS OUT, I WAS TOO OLD TO BE IN CLINICAL TRIALS DUE TO THE RULES THE PHARMACEUTICAL COMPANIES MAKE.
COULD YOU IMAGINE? THEY HAVE TENS OF THOUSANDS OF VIALS OF VYONDYS 53 SITTING IN A WAREHOUSE. AND THERE WAS NOTHING I COULD DO ABOUT IT.
MY PARENTS WOULD WRITE LETTER AFTER LETTER...
DENIED
DENIED
TO MAKE MATTERS WORSE, ONCE THE DRUG GOT APPROVED...
DENIED
DENIED
THE INSURANCE COMPANY DENIED ME...
THEY WOULD WRITE LETTER AFTER LETTER...
DENIED
AND STILL... DENIED.
SO LET ME GET THIS STRAIGHT...
I'M TOO OLD FOR CLINICAL TRIALS... THEN YOU APPROVE THE DRUG FOR USAGE... AND NOW THE INSURANCE COMPANY SAYS "NO."

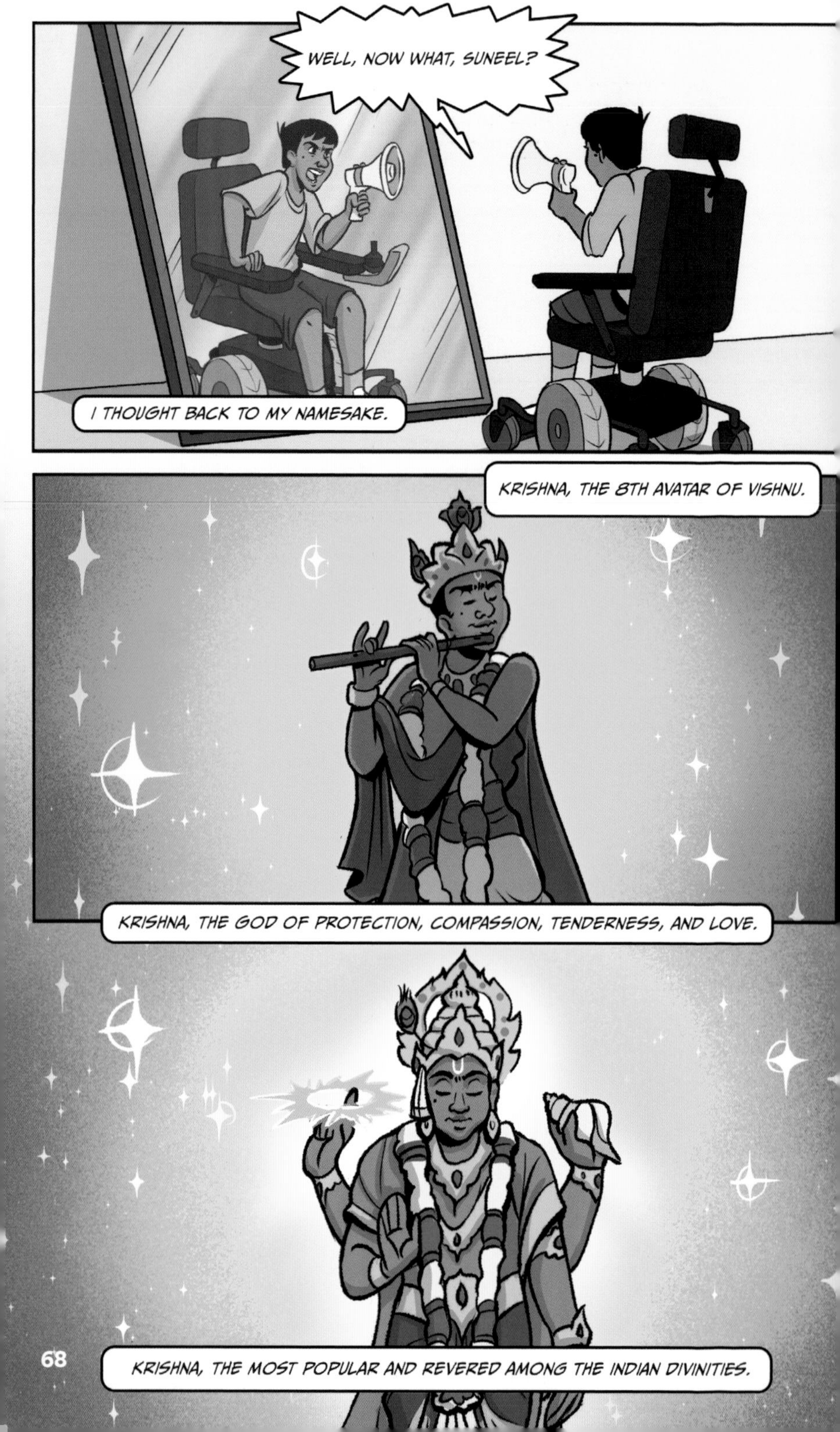
WELL, NOW WHAT, SUNEEL?
I THOUGHT BACK TO MY NAMESAKE.
KRISHNA, THE 8TH AVATAR OF VISHNU.
KRISHNA, THE GOD OF PROTECTION, COMPASSION, TENDERNESS, AND LOVE.
KRISHNA, THE MOST POPULAR AND REVERED AMONG THE INDIAN DIVINITIES.

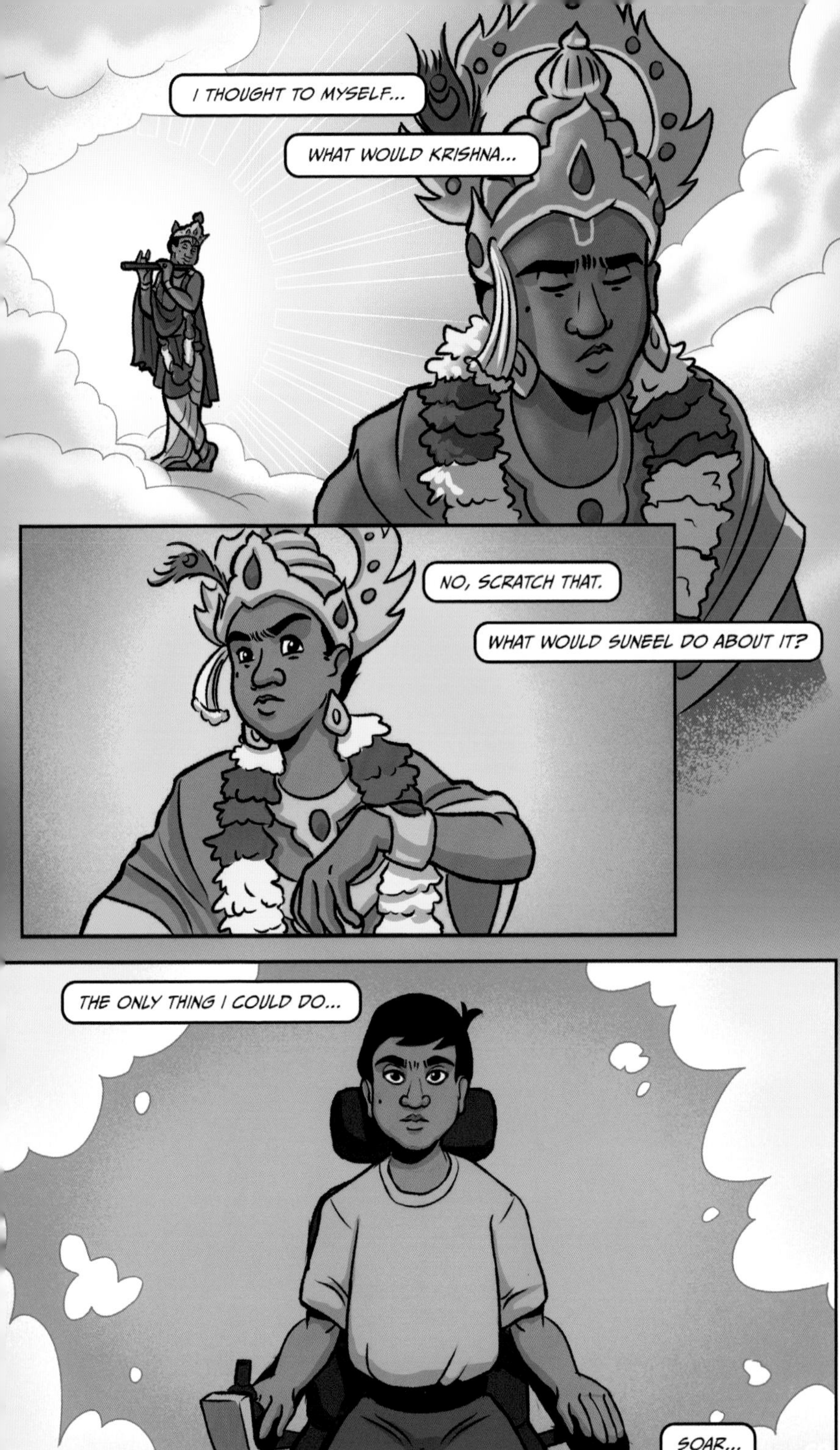
I THOUGHT TO MYSELF...
WHAT WOULD KRISHNA...
NO, SCRATCH THAT.
WHAT WOULD SUNEEL DO ABOUT IT?
THE ONLY THING I COULD DO...
SOAR...

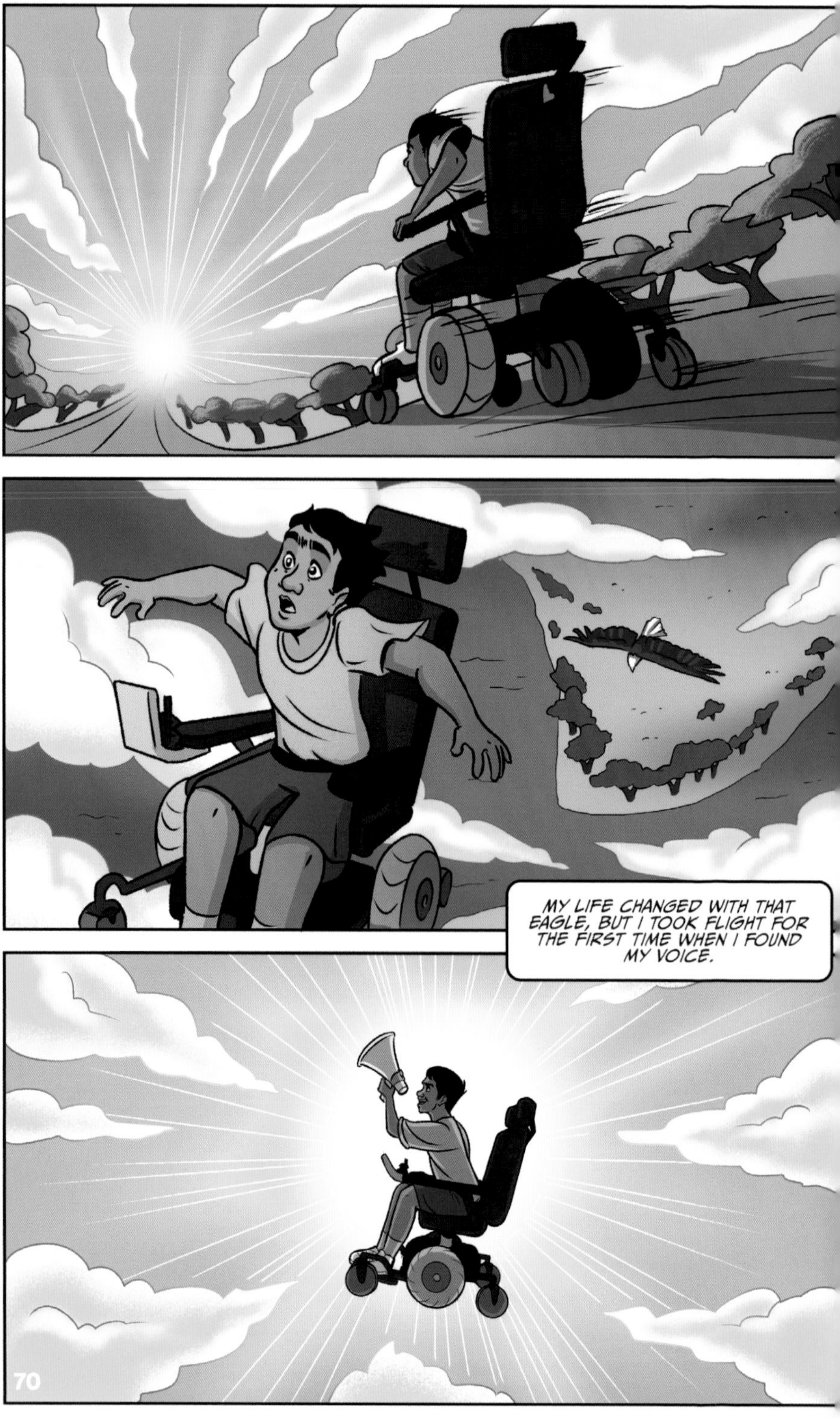
MY LIFE CHANGED WITH THAT EAGLE, BUT I TOOK FLIGHT FOR THE FIRST TIME WHEN I FOUND MY VOICE.

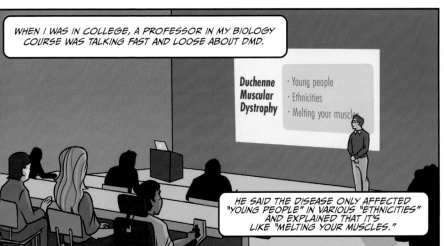

WHEN I WAS IN COLLEGE, A PROFESSOR IN MY BIOLOGY COURSE WAS TALKING FAST AND LOOSE ABOUT DMD.

Duchenne Muscular Dystrophy
- Young people
- Ethnicities
- Melting your muscles

HE SAID THE DISEASE ONLY AFFECTED "YOUNG PEOPLE" IN VARIOUS "ETHNICITIES" AND EXPLAINED THAT IT'S LIKE "MELTING YOUR MUSCLES."

UNDERSTAND THIS. I NEVER TOLD ANYONE IN COLLEGE I HAD DMD.

I WAS JUST ANOTHER STUDENT IN THE CLASS WHO HAPPENED TO BE IN A WHEELCHAIR.

I WAS CRUSHED THAT AN EDUCATOR COULD BE SO MISINFORMED ABOUT WHAT I LIVE WITH EVERY DAY.

SO, I WENT HOME AND ASKED MY AIDE TO HELP ME CRAFT A RESPONSE.

SHE GRABBED A HANDFUL OF NOTE CARDS AND A COUPLE OF MARKERS.

THE NEXT DAY I SPOKE IN FRONT OF THE CLASS.

THE SPEECH, ON NOTE CARDS, WENT A LITTLE SOMETHING LIKE THIS...

71

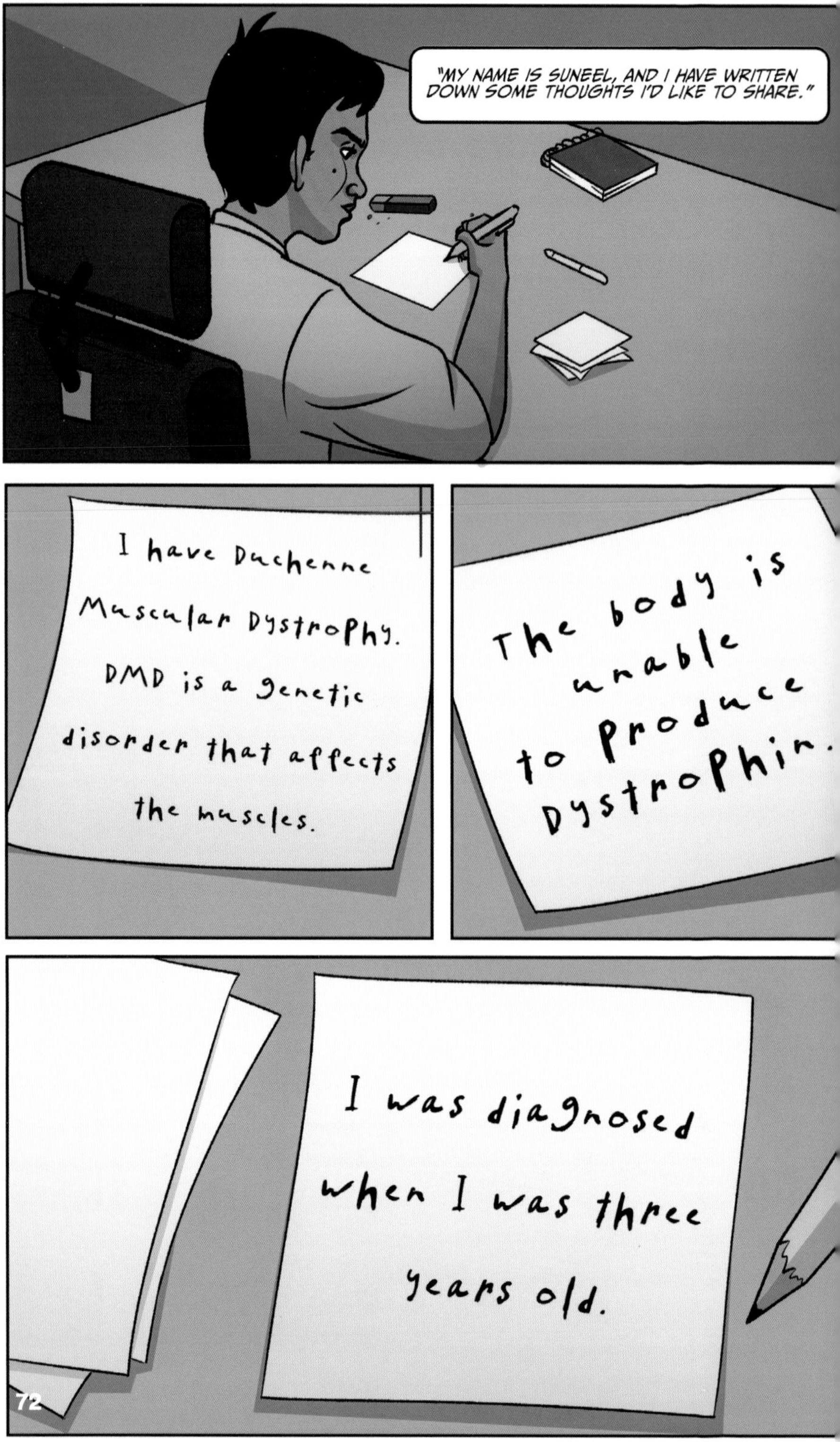

"MY NAME IS SUNEEL, AND I HAVE WRITTEN DOWN SOME THOUGHTS I'D LIKE TO SHARE."
I have Duchenne Muscular Dystrophy. DMD is a genetic disorder that affects the muscles.
The body is unable to produce Dystrophin.
I was diagnosed when I was three years old.

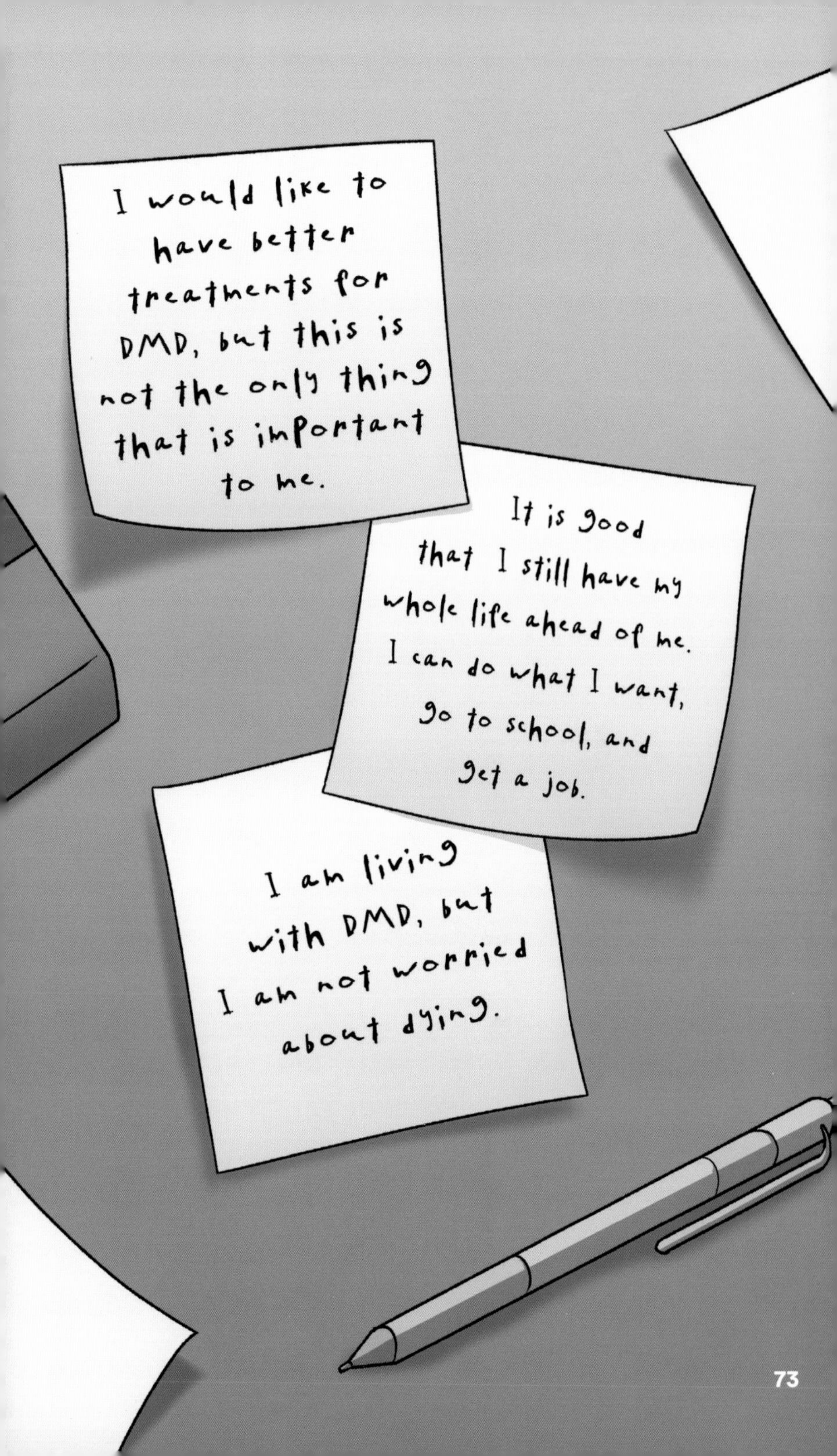
I would like to have better treatments for DMD, but this is not the only thing that is important to me.
It is good that I still have my whole life ahead of me. I can do what I want, go to school, and get a job.
I am living with DMD, but I am not worried about dying.

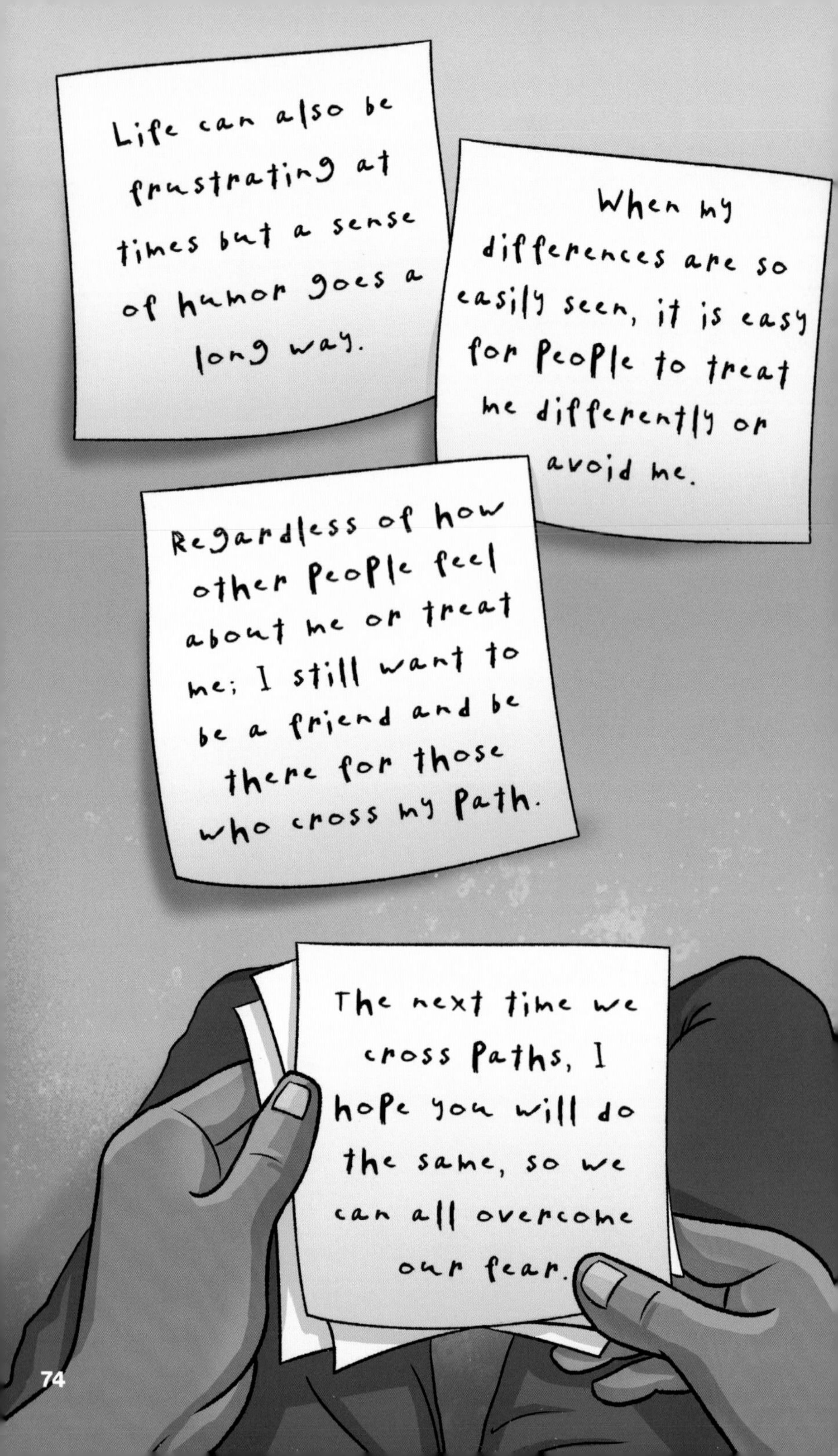
Life can also be frustrating at times but a sense of humor goes a long way.
When my differences are so easily seen, it is easy for people to treat me differently or avoid me.
Regardless of how other people feel about me or treat me; I still want to be a friend and be there for those who cross my path.
The next time we cross paths, I hope you will do the same, so we can all overcome our fear.

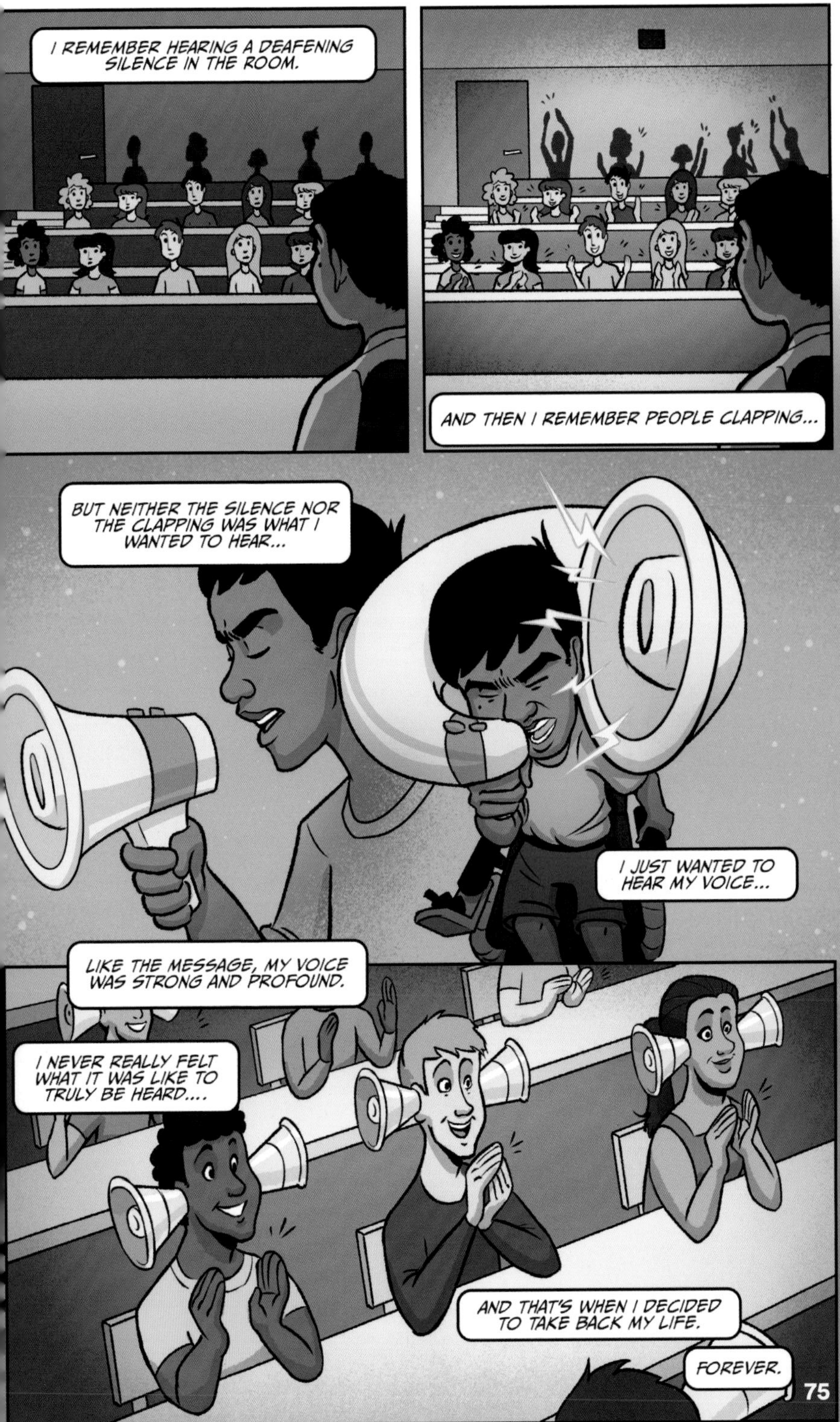
I REMEMBER HEARING A DEAFENING SILENCE IN THE ROOM.
AND THEN I REMEMBER PEOPLE CLAPPING...
BUT NEITHER THE SILENCE NOR THE CLAPPING WAS WHAT I WANTED TO HEAR...
I JUST WANTED TO HEAR MY VOICE...
LIKE THE MESSAGE, MY VOICE WAS STRONG AND PROFOUND.
I NEVER REALLY FELT WHAT IT WAS LIKE TO TRULY BE HEARD....
AND THAT'S WHEN I DECIDED TO TAKE BACK MY LIFE.
FOREVER.

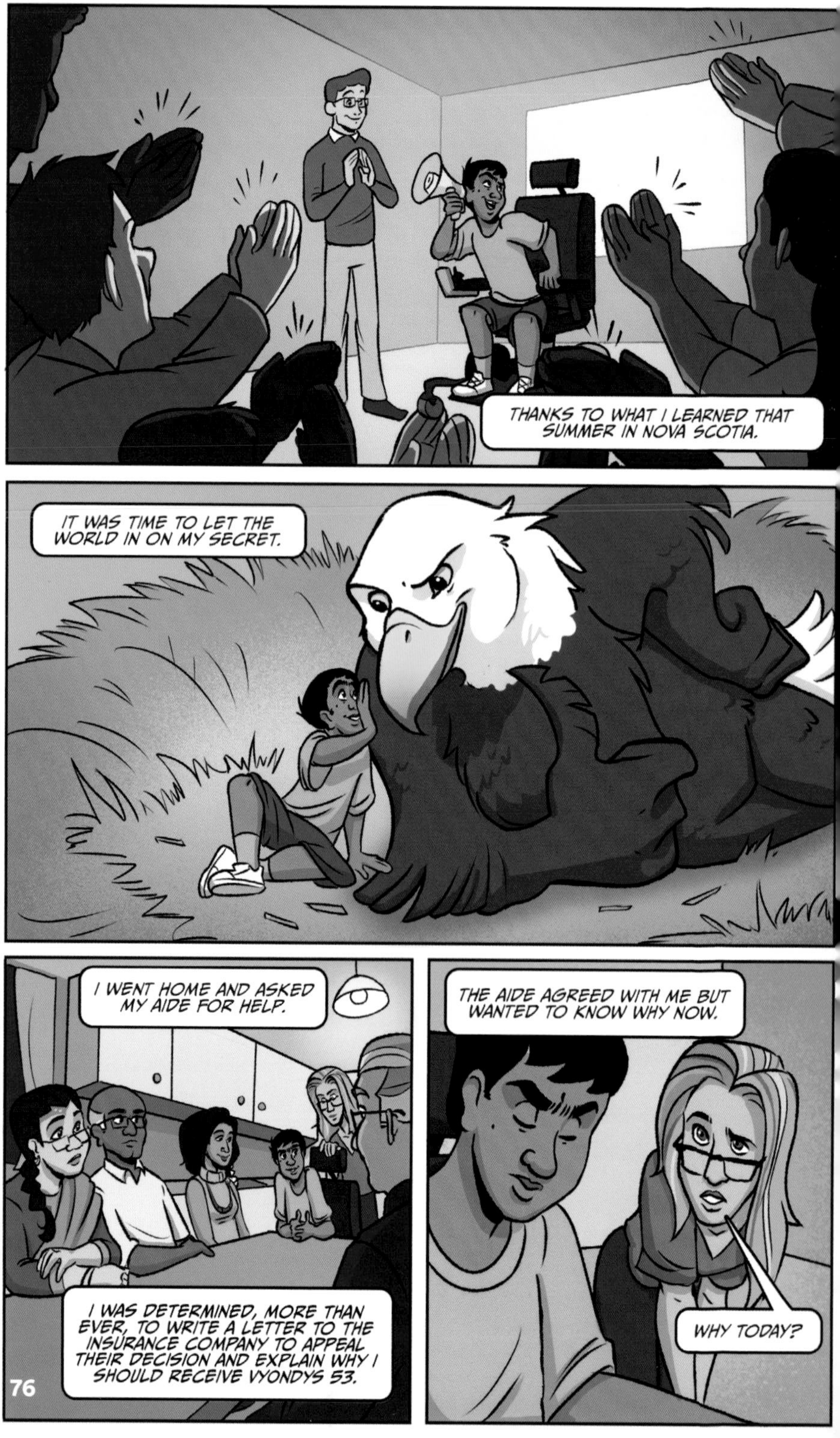
THANKS TO WHAT I LEARNED THAT SUMMER IN NOVA SCOTIA.
IT WAS TIME TO LET THE WORLD IN ON MY SECRET.
I WENT HOME AND ASKED MY AIDE FOR HELP.
I WAS DETERMINED, MORE THAN EVER, TO WRITE A LETTER TO THE INSURANCE COMPANY TO APPEAL THEIR DECISION AND EXPLAIN WHY I SHOULD RECEIVE VYONDYS 53.
THE AIDE AGREED WITH ME BUT WANTED TO KNOW WHY NOW.
WHY TODAY?

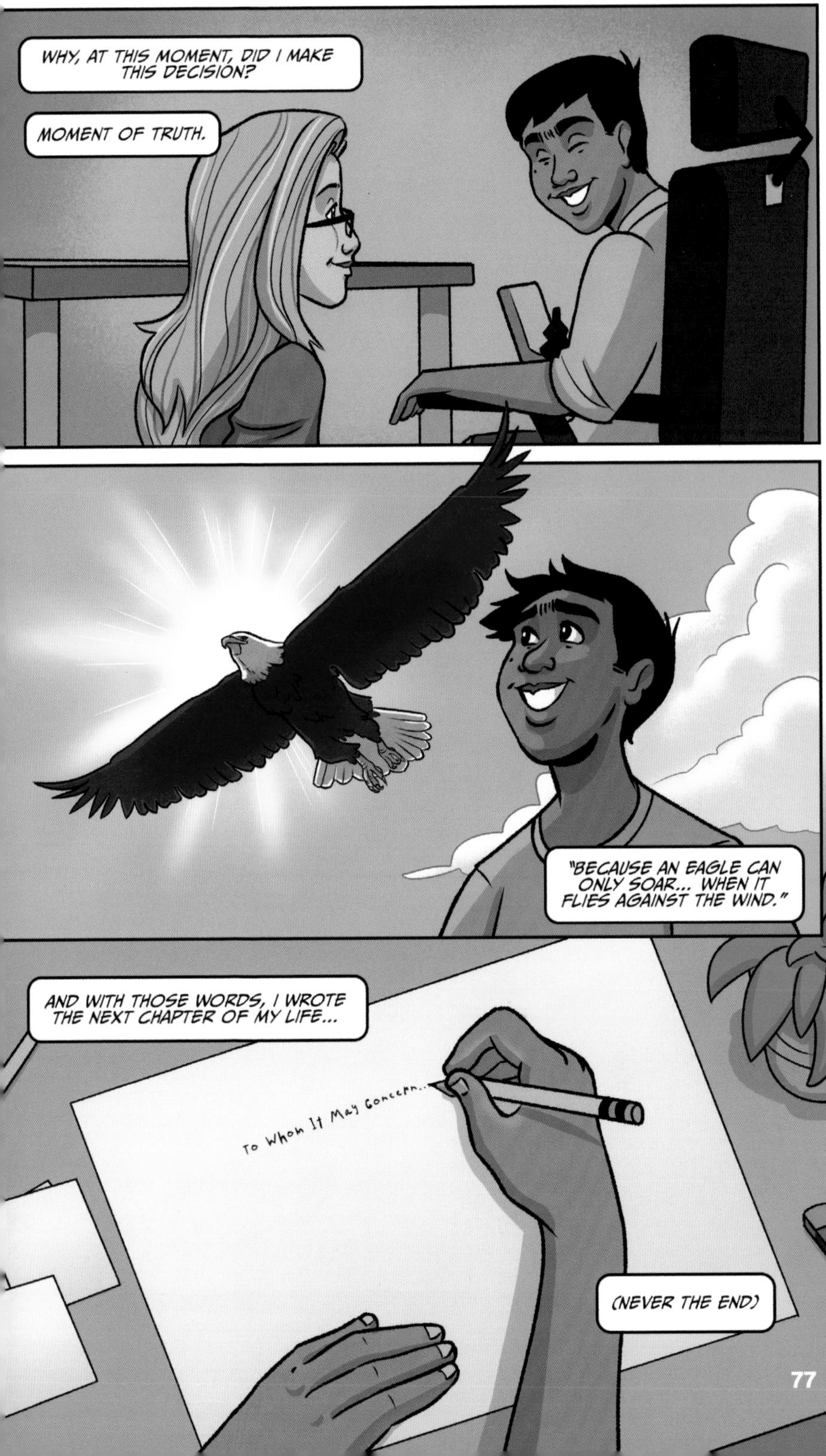
WHY, AT THIS MOMENT, DID I MAKE THIS DECISION?
MOMENT OF TRUTH.
"BECAUSE AN EAGLE CAN ONLY SOAR... WHEN IT FLIES AGAINST THE WIND."
AND WITH THOSE WORDS, I WROTE THE NEXT CHAPTER OF MY LIFE...
To Whom It May Concern...
(NEVER THE END)

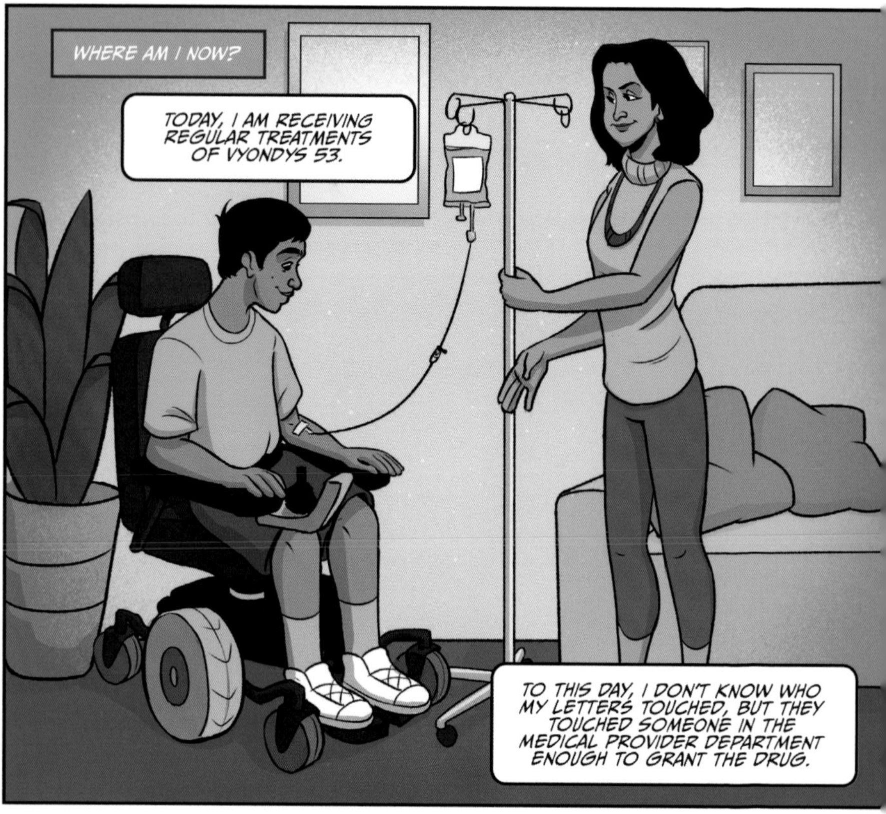
WHERE AM I NOW?
TODAY, I AM RECEIVING REGULAR TREATMENTS OF VYONDYS 53.
TO THIS DAY, I DON'T KNOW WHO MY LETTERS TOUCHED, BUT THEY TOUCHED SOMEONE IN THE MEDICAL PROVIDER DEPARTMENT ENOUGH TO GRANT THE DRUG.

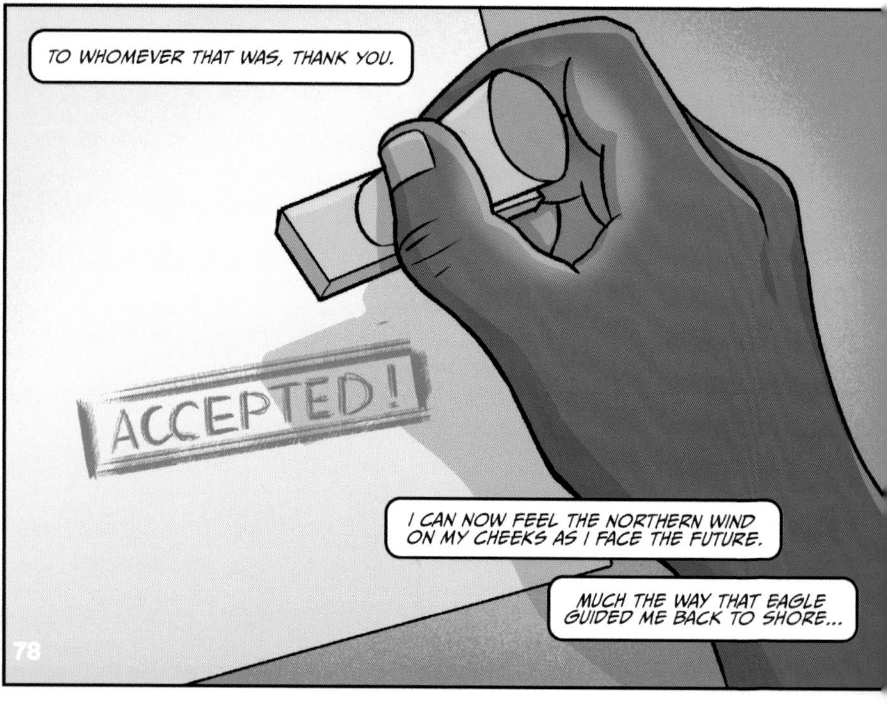
TO WHOMEVER THAT WAS, THANK YOU.
ACCEPTED!
I CAN NOW FEEL THE NORTHERN WIND ON MY CHEEKS AS I FACE THE FUTURE.
MUCH THE WAY THAT EAGLE GUIDED ME BACK TO SHORE...

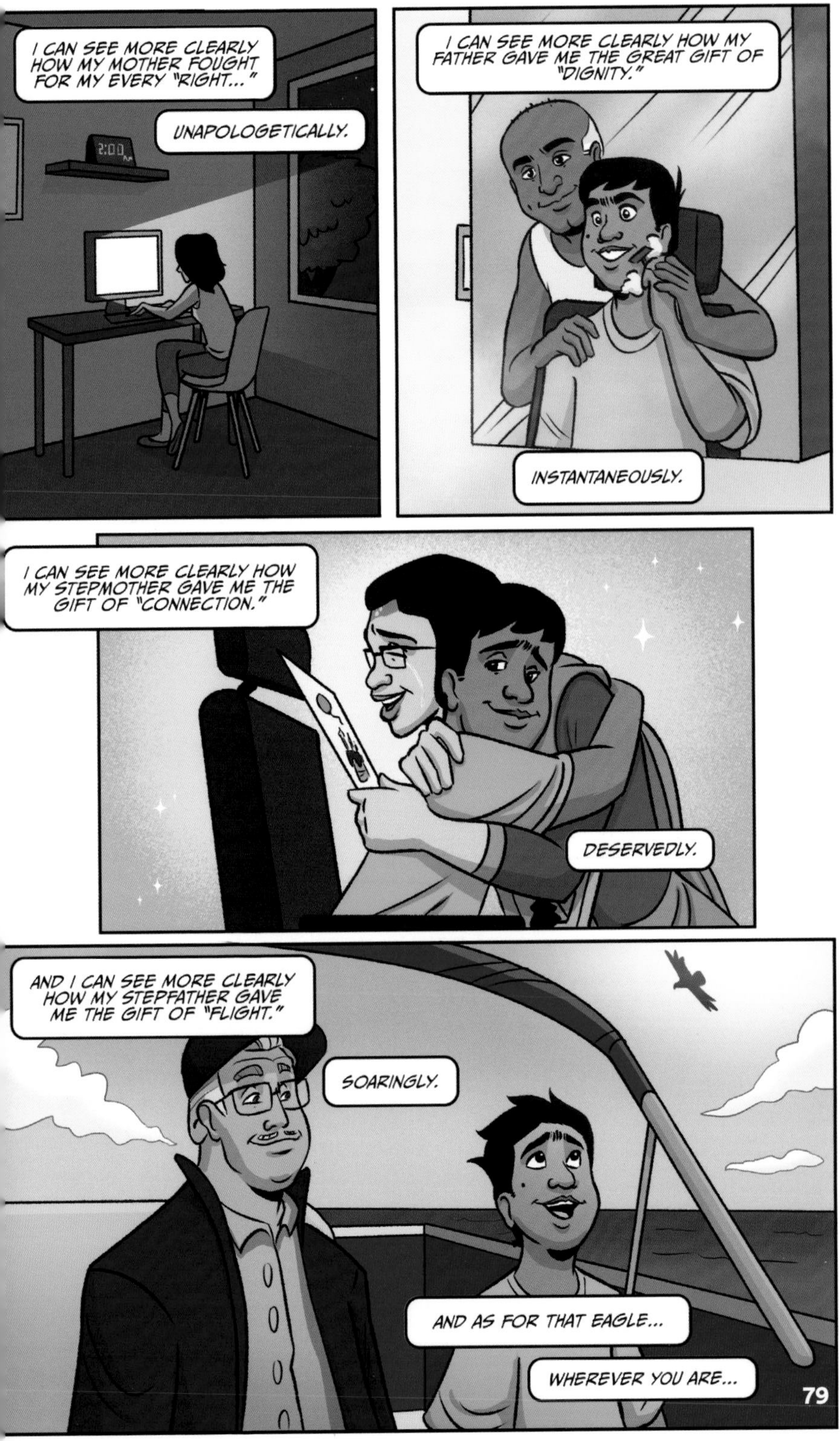
I CAN SEE MORE CLEARLY HOW MY MOTHER FOUGHT FOR MY EVERY "RIGHT..."
UNAPOLOGETICALLY.
I CAN SEE MORE CLEARLY HOW MY FATHER GAVE ME THE GREAT GIFT OF "DIGNITY."
INSTANTANEOUSLY.
I CAN SEE MORE CLEARLY HOW MY STEPMOTHER GAVE ME THE GIFT OF "CONNECTION."
DESERVEDLY.
AND I CAN SEE MORE CLEARLY HOW MY STEPFATHER GAVE ME THE GIFT OF "FLIGHT."
SOARINGLY.
AND AS FOR THAT EAGLE...
WHEREVER YOU ARE...

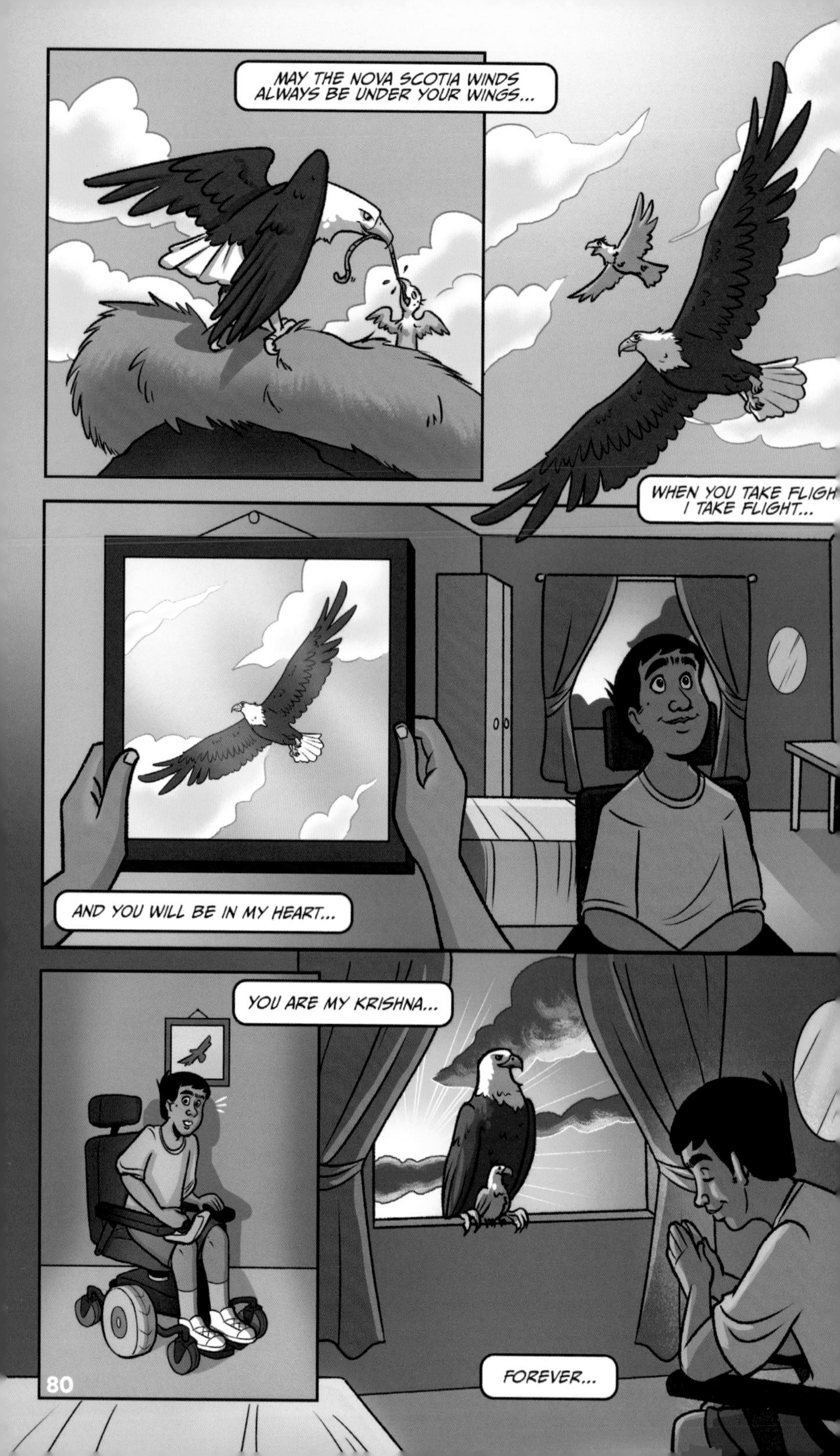

MAY THE NOVA SCOTIA WINDS ALWAYS BE UNDER YOUR WINGS...
WHEN YOU TAKE FLIGH
I TAKE FLIGHT...
AND YOU WILL BE IN MY HEART...
YOU ARE MY KRISHNA...
FOREVER...

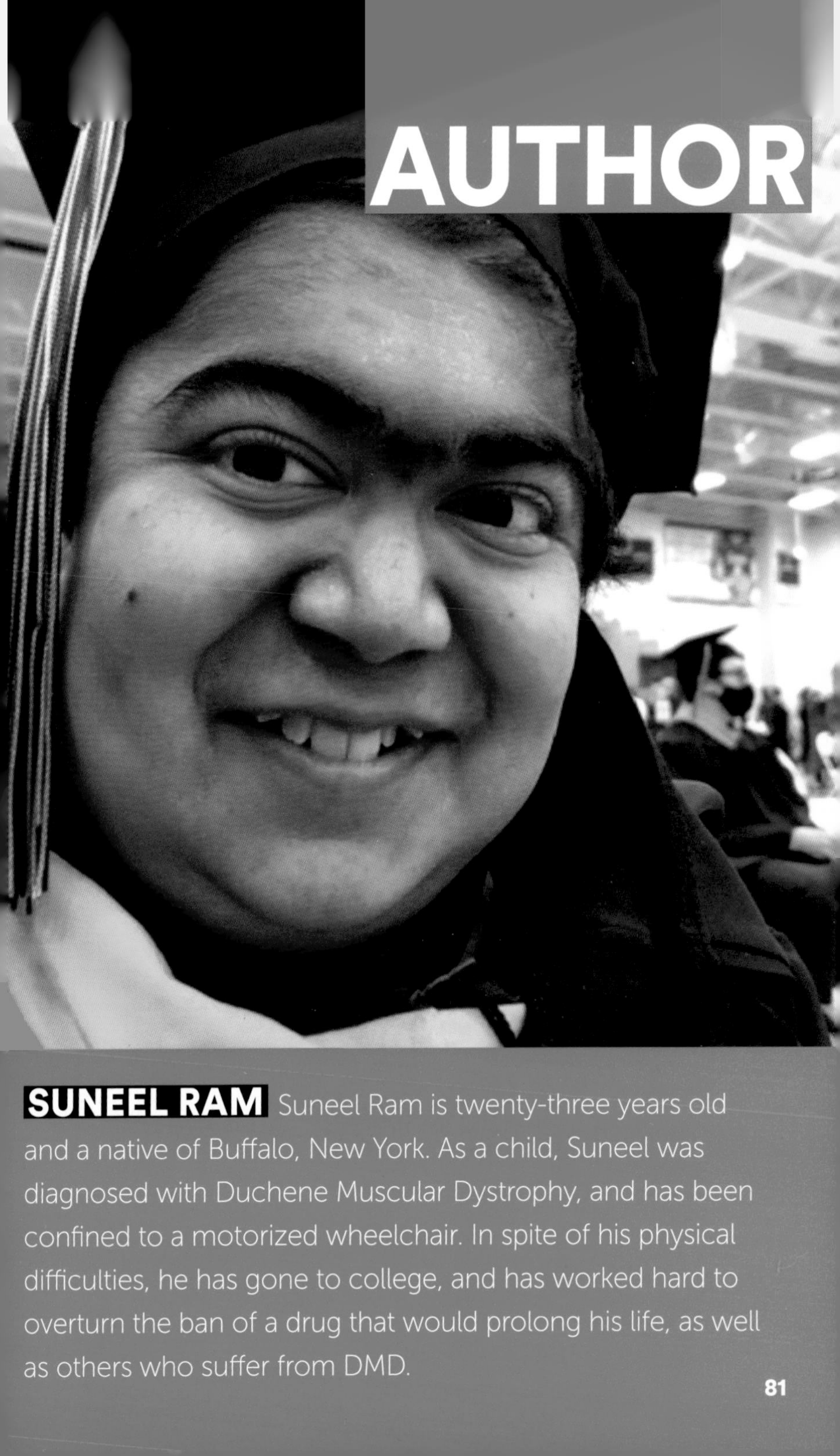

AUTHOR

SUNEEL RAM Suneel Ram is twenty-three years old and a native of Buffalo, New York. As a child, Suneel was diagnosed with Duchene Muscular Dystrophy, and has been confined to a motorized wheelchair. In spite of his physical difficulties, he has gone to college, and has worked hard to overturn the ban of a drug that would prolong his life, as well as others who suffer from DMD.

SUNEEL...

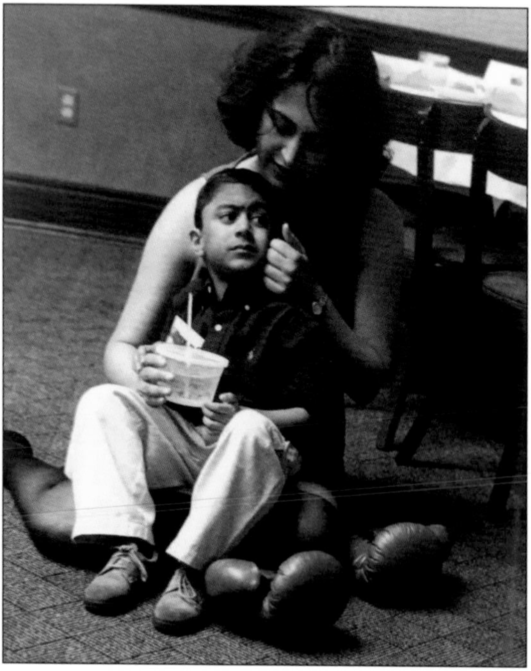

This is my mother and me. I chose this picture because I'm a fighter and my mom is always in my corner.

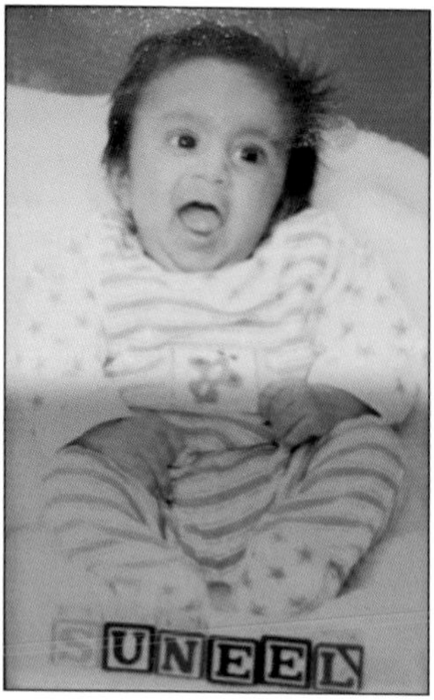
SUNEEL

Look out world! Here comes baby Suneel. Check out my wooden letters.

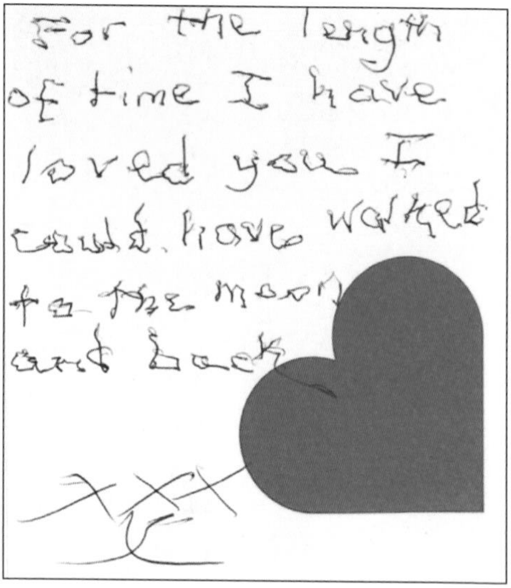
For the length of time I have loved you I could have walked to the moon and back

I hand wrote words to my parents that came straight from my heart.

SUNEEL...

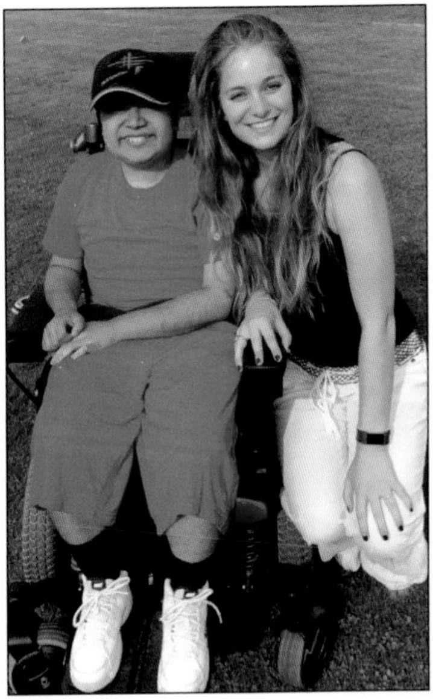

This is my friend Beth by my side. Always.

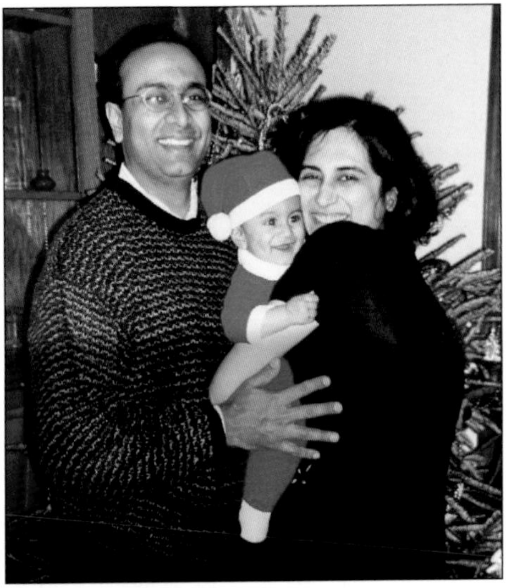

This is my mom and dad making me a Santa sandwich.

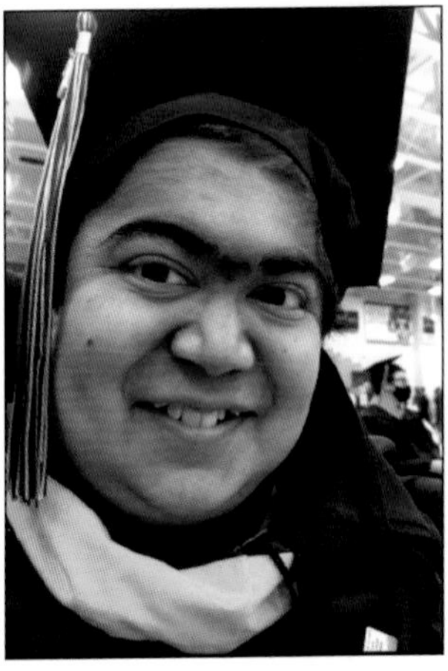

This is me graduating from Canisius college.

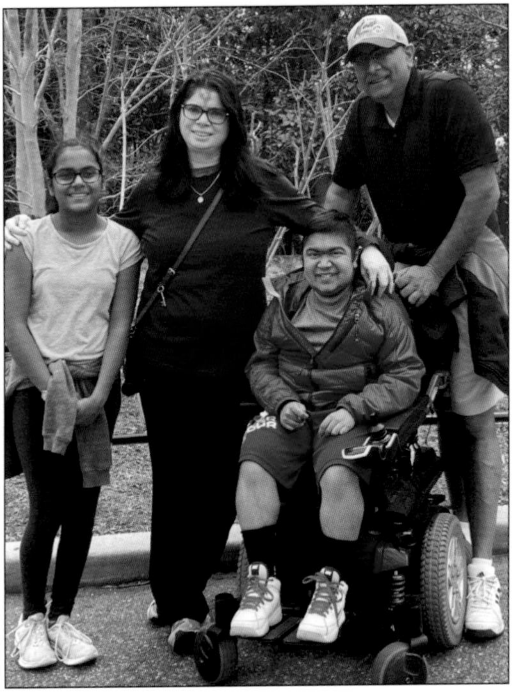

My awesome family. Dad, PK, sister Nandini, and me (and Janani taking the picture).

SUNEEL...

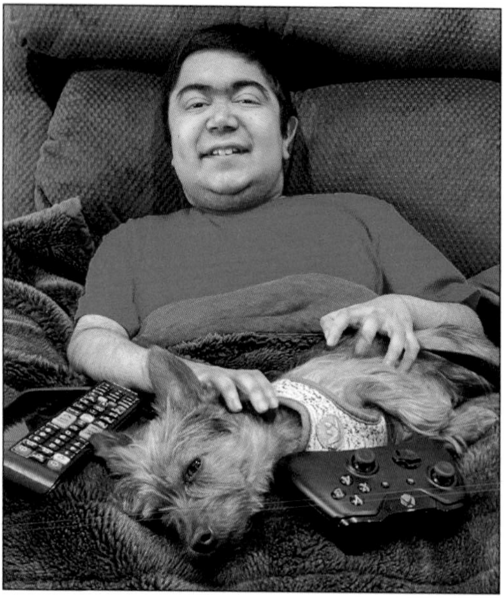

This is my dog Thor after I beat him in XBox.

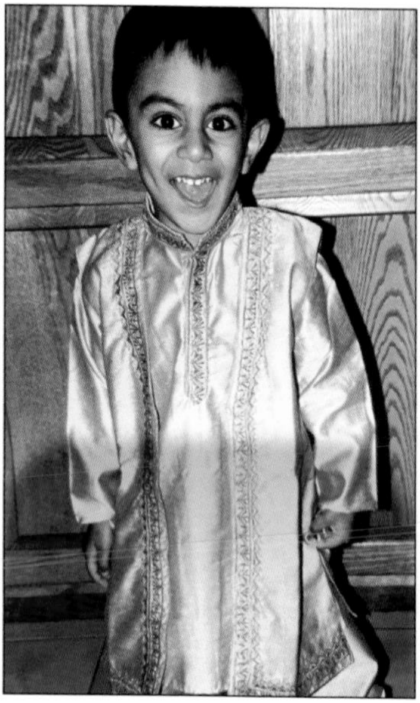

Check me out sporting my kurta pajamas.

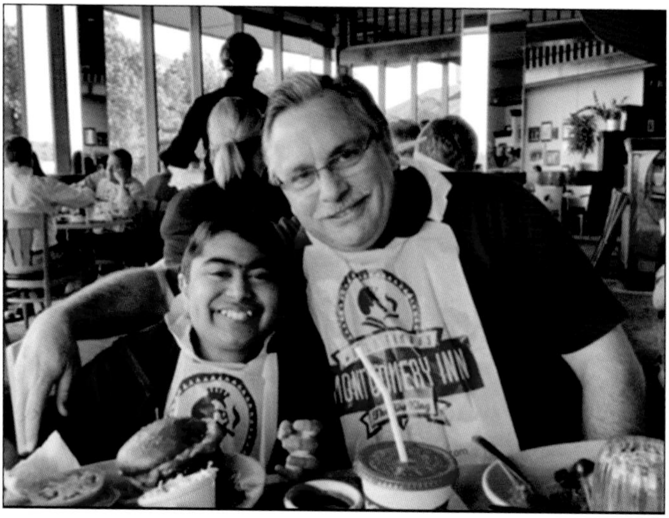

My stepfather, Ken, and me eating at Montgomery Inn.

TAKE 5!

FIVE PARENT TAKE-AWAYS ABOUT DMD

NEERA GULATI is Suneel Ram's mother, family medicine physician, and Founder of nonprofit foundation Suneel's Light, whose mission is increasing awareness of Duchenne Muscular Dystrophy and supporting medical research for effective treatments and cure.

DUCHENNE MUSCULAR DYSTROPHY (DMD) IS A RARE GENETIC DISORDER characterized by progressive muscle degeneration and weakness due to mutations in a protein called dystrophin. Dystrophin is essential for muscles to function. It acts like a shock absorber when muscles contract. Without dystrophin, muscles become damaged and weakened, and are replaced with fat and fibrous tissue. This progressive muscular weakness leads to loss of mobility, and eventually ability to breathe. It affects mostly boys, but girls can be carriers. It's estimated at 1:3200 male births.

AN INFANT WITH DMD MAY APPEAR TO BE FLOPPY, WITH POOR MUSCLE CONTROL OF THE HEAD AND NECK. He will present delayed motor milestones, such as sitting up, crawling, standing, and walking. Other signs include using his hands to push on his legs to go from sitting to standing; a waddling gait; difficulty running, jumping, and climbing stairs; difficulty with motor skills; abnormal hypertrophy of calf muscles; and learning disabilities.

ALTHOUGH THERE IS NO CURE YET, it's important to see a neurologist who is well versed in DMD and begin the treatment, Deflazacort, as soon as the diagnosis is established. Find out the exact genetic mutation. Based on

his mutation, your child may be able to start on new treatments to slow the disease, such as exon-skipping drugs. Connect with foundations, such as: Jett Foundation; Charley's Fund; Cure Duchenne; and Parent Project Muscular Dystrophy for valuable information for daily living and for available clinical trials.

MAKE SURE YOUR CHILD UNDERSTANDS THAT HE HAS TO PROTECT HIS MUSCLES AND BONES. That is why he takes medications that will make him short and a little hairy. Classmates, peers, and family members also should be educated on the importance of this protection, and on the side effects of medications. Be honest and give examples of how DMD affects your child's daily activities to help them foster empathy. Adapt activities so your child is not at risk. Most important, talk to school, family members, and peers about being inclusive and compassionate. Adapting is not excluding. Exclusion hurts and is lonely.

FIND OUT THE EXACT MUTATION OF DYSTROPHIN GENE. Ask your neurologist if your child can take any of the new exon-skipping drugs. Foster connections with DMD Foundations to stay up to date on treatment and options to ensure child receives best possible care.

THE STORY DOESN'T END HERE...

VISIT
ZUIKERPRESS.COM

... to learn more about Suneel's story, see behind-the-scenes videos of Suneel and his family, and to learn more about DMD.

Our **WEBSITE** is another resource to help our readers deal with the issues that they face every day. Log on to find advice from experts, links to helpful organizations and literature, and more real-life experiences from young people just like you.

Spotlighting young writers with heartfelt stories that enlighten and inspire.

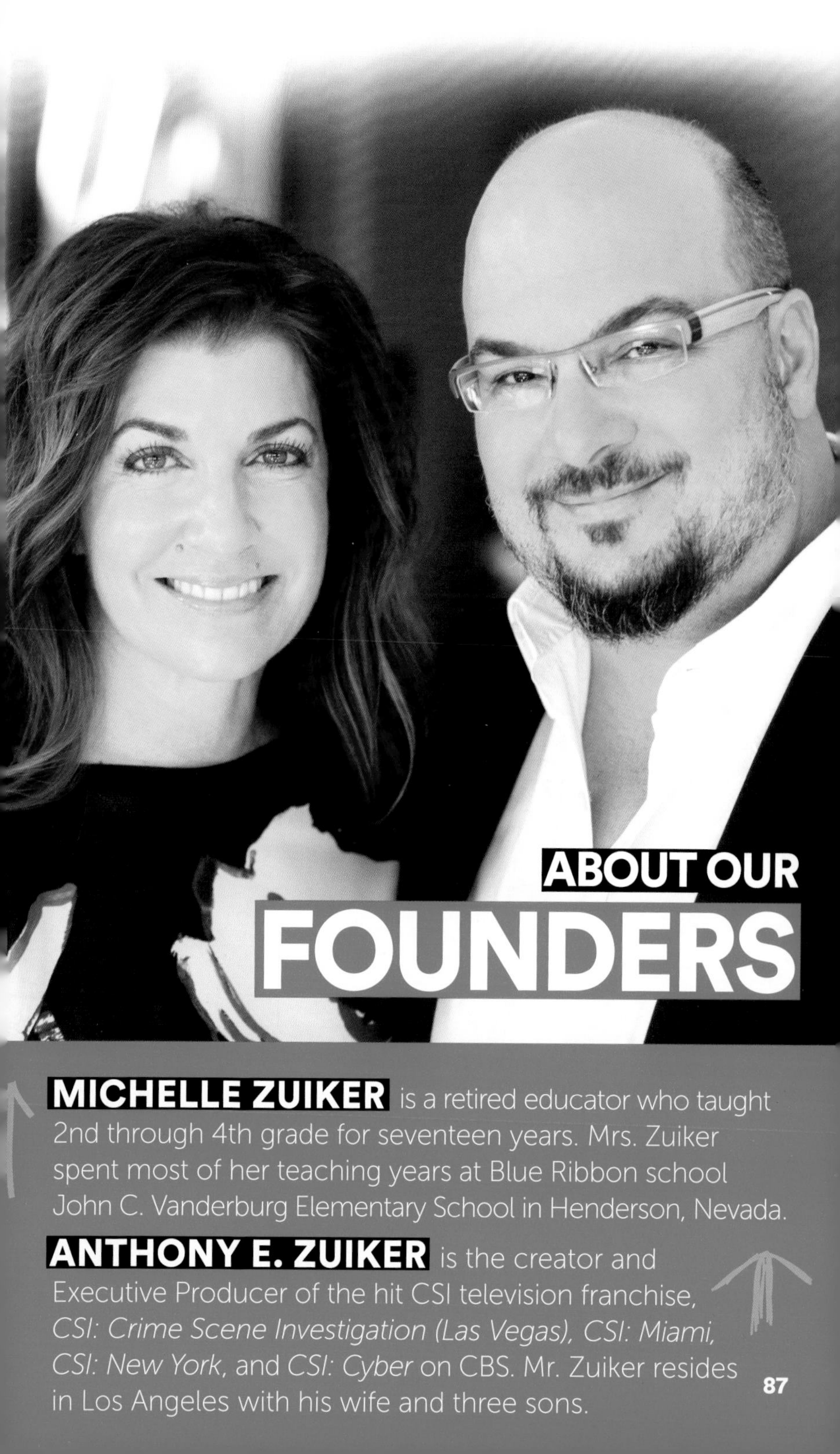

ABOUT OUR FOUNDERS

MICHELLE ZUIKER is a retired educator who taught 2nd through 4th grade for seventeen years. Mrs. Zuiker spent most of her teaching years at Blue Ribbon school John C. Vanderburg Elementary School in Henderson, Nevada.

ANTHONY E. ZUIKER is the creator and Executive Producer of the hit CSI television franchise, *CSI: Crime Scene Investigation (Las Vegas)*, *CSI: Miami*, *CSI: New York*, and *CSI: Cyber* on CBS. Mr. Zuiker resides in Los Angeles with his wife and three sons.

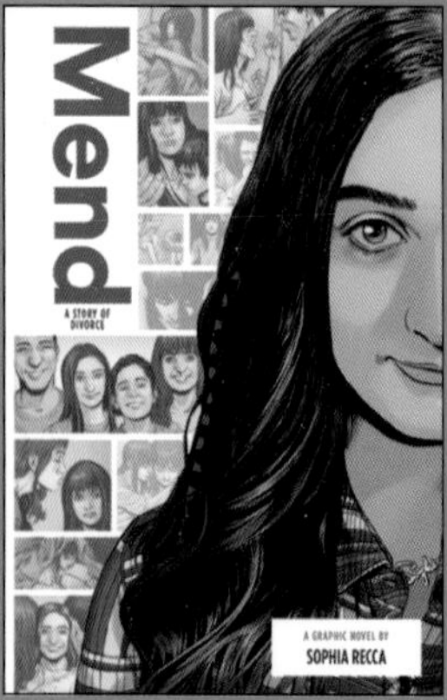
Mend
A STORY OF DIVORCE
A GRAPHIC NOVEL BY
SOPHIA RECCA

MEND: A STORY OF DIVORCE
APPROVED FOR SCHOOL USE
ISBN: 978-1-947378-00-1 HC $12.99
ISBN: 978-1-947378-02-5 EB $7.99

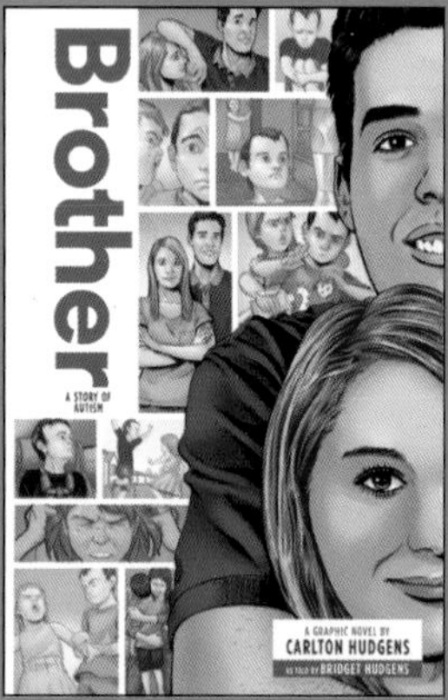
Brother
A STORY OF AUTISM
A GRAPHIC NOVEL BY
CARLTON HUDGENS
AS TOLD BY BRIDGET HUDGENS

BROTHER: A STORY OF AUTISM
APPROVED FOR SCHOOL USE
ISBN: 978-1-947378-08-7 HC $12.99
ISBN: 978-1-947378-10-0 EB $7.99

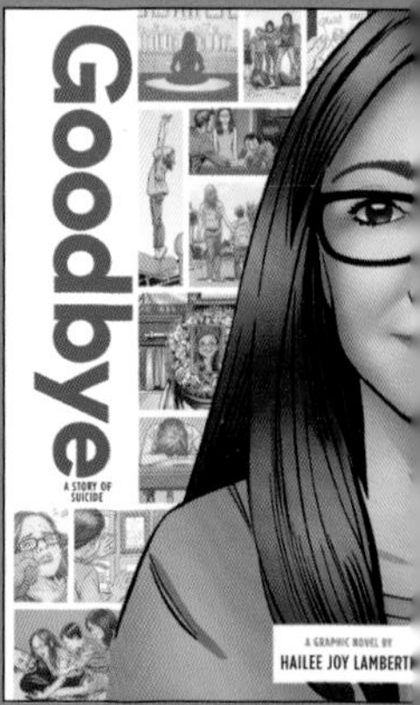
Goodbye
A STORY OF SUICIDE
A GRAPHIC NOVEL BY
HAILEE JOY LAMBERT

GOODBYE: A STORY OF SUICIDE
ISBN: 978-1-947378-27-8 HC $12
ISBN: 978-1-947378-29-2 EB $7.9

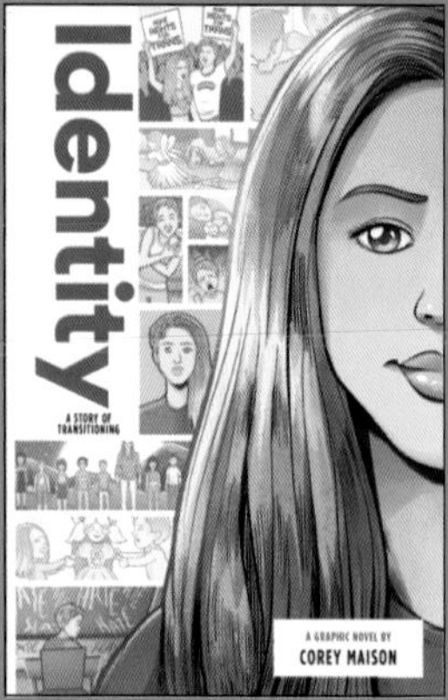
Identity
A STORY OF TRANSITIONING
A GRAPHIC NOVEL BY
COREY MAISON

IDENTITY: A STORY OF TRANSITIONING
APPROVED FOR SCHOOL USE
ISBN: 978-1-947378-24-7 HC $12.99
ISBN: 978-1-947378-26-1 EB $7.99

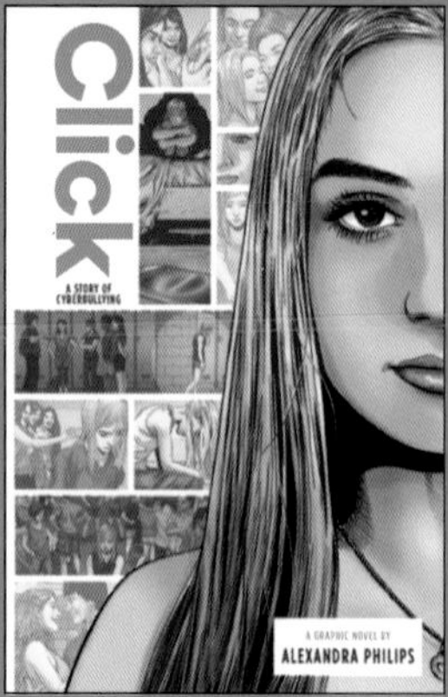
Click
A STORY OF CYBERBULLYING
A GRAPHIC NOVEL BY
ALEXANDRA PHILIPS

CLICK: A STORY OF CYBERBULLYING
APPROVED FOR SCHOOL USE
ISBN: 978-1-947378-04-9 HC $12.99
ISBN: 978-1-947378-06-3 EB $7.99

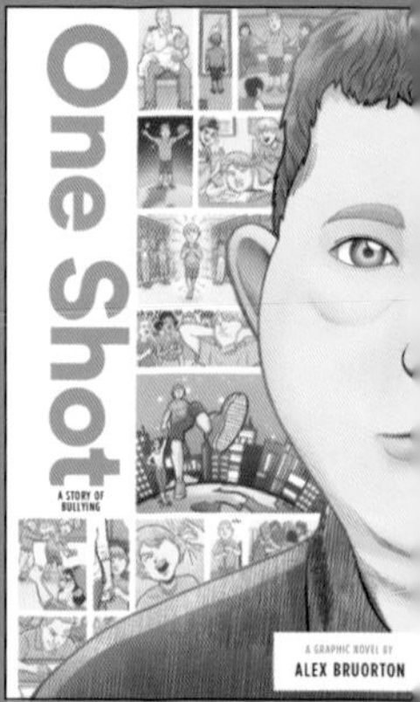
One Shot
A STORY OF BULLYING
A GRAPHIC NOVEL BY
ALEX BRUORTON

ONE SHOT: A STORY OF BULLYING
APPROVED FOR SCHOOL USE
ISBN 978-1-947378-30-8 HC $12.
ISBN 978-1-947378-32-2 EB $7.99

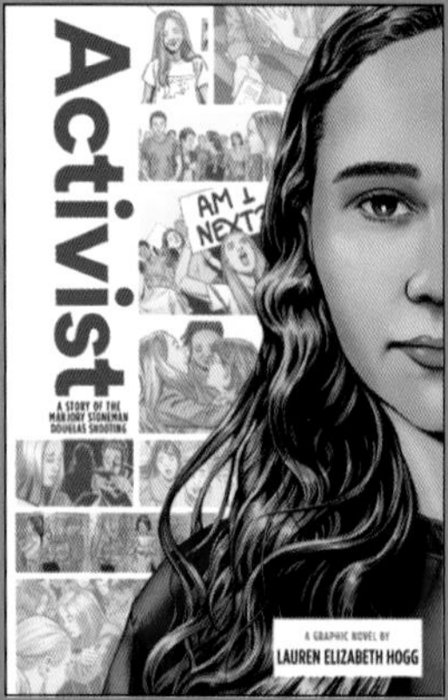
Activist
A STORY OF THE MARJORY STONEMAN DOUGLAS SHOOTING
AM I NEXT?
A GRAPHIC NOVEL BY
LAUREN ELIZABETH HOGG

ACTIVIST: A STORY OF THE MARJORY STONEMAN DOUGLAS SHOOTING
ISBN: 978-1-947378-21-6 HC $12.99
ISBN: 978-1-947378-23-0 EB $7.99
APPROVED FOR SCHOOL USE
ISBN: 978-1-947378-37-7 PB $9.99

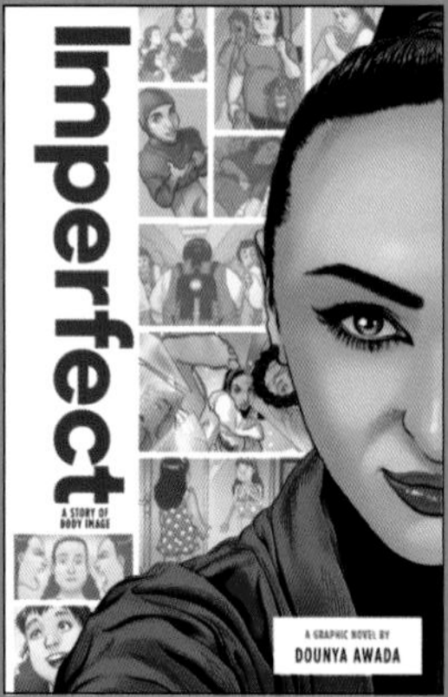
Imperfect
A STORY OF BODY IMAGE
A GRAPHIC NOVEL BY
DOUNYA AWADA

IMPERFECT: A STORY OF BODY IMAGE
ISBN: 978-1-947387-07-0 HC $12.99
ISBN: 978-1-947378-03-2 EB $7.99
APPROVED FOR SCHOOL USE
ISBN: 978-1-947378-38-4 PB $9.99

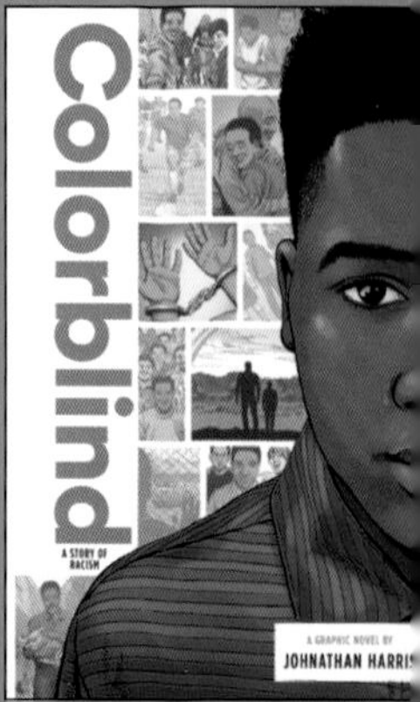
Colorblind
A STORY OF RACISM
A GRAPHIC NOVEL BY
JOHNATHAN HARRIS

COLORBLIND: A STORY OF RACISM
ISBN: 978-1-947378-12-4 HC $12
ISBN: 978-1-947378-14-8 EB $7.9
APPROVED FOR SCHOOL USE
ISBN: 978-1-947378-37-7 PB $9.9